Into His Likeness

Be Transformed
as a Disciple of Christ

By Edward Sri

Ignatius Press   Augustine Institute
San Francisco   Greenwood Village, CO

Ignatius Press Distribution
1915 Aster Rd.
Sycamore, IL 60178
Tel: (630) 246-2204
www.ignatius.com

Augustine Institute
6160 S. Syracuse Way, Suite 310
Greenwood Village, CO 80111
Tel: (866) 767-3155
www.augustineinstitute.org

Cover Design: Ben Dybas

Photograph of author by K Caulfield Photography

ISBN: 978-0-9993756-5-5
Library of Congress Control Number 2017958991

Printed in the United States

To my son, Paul

TABLE OF CONTENTS

And we all, with unveiled face, beholding the glory of the Lord, are being changed into his likeness from one degree of glory to another; for this comes from the Lord who is the Spirit.

—2 Corinthians 3:18

"DO YOU LOVE ME?"

Introduction

On a spring morning along the Sea of Galilee some 2,000 years ago, the Risen Jesus asks his disciple Peter this deeply personal question: "Do you love me?"

At first glance, we might expect Peter to give a whole-hearted "Yes!" After all, Peter was one of Jesus's first disciples. He had left his fishing nets behind and made many sacrifices to follow Jesus for the last three years. Moreover, Jesus selected Peter as one of the Twelve Apostles to whom he entrusted his mission of proclaiming the Kingdom of God. To top it off, Peter was the first to confess explicitly that Jesus was the Messiah and as a result was given the keys of the kingdom, symbolizing his special role of leadership among the Twelve.

That's why Jesus's question "Do you love me?" seems on the surface to be a no-brainer. Of course Peter loves Jesus! Peter the Fisherman-Turned-Disciple, Peter the Chosen Apostle, Peter the First Pope—surely *he* would be a model of faithfulness!

But the word Jesus uses for "love" here makes Peter pause. The Gospel of John employs the Greek word *agapao*, which describes total, unconditional, self-giving love—the kind of committed, sacrificial love Jesus models throughout his life, most especially on the Cross. Jesus, therefore, is not asking Peter if he loves merely with ordinary human affection. Another Greek word, *phileo*, tends to describe that kind of love—the love of friendship, tender but not all-encompassing.[1] Rather, Peter is being asked if he loves as Christ loves. Does Peter love Jesus with *agape* love?[2]

At this, Peter holds back. He knows he can't go there. He sadly wishes he could say yes, and in the past his naïve overzealousness may have led him to do so. In fact, not too long ago, Peter even boldly pledged his absolute fidelity to Jesus, saying at the Last Supper, "Lord, I am ready to go with you to prison and to death" (Lk 22:33). But his threefold denial of Christ later that same night makes Peter's shortcomings in *agape* painfully clear. Peter gives in to fear, betrays his friend three times, and turns away weeping bitterly when he realizes what he has done. He has tasted the bitter sorrow of his weakness and infidelity.

So now, a much more humbled Peter qualifies his affirmation of love. He admits to Jesus, "Lord, you know that I love you (*phileo*)." It's as if Peter is saying, "You of all people, Jesus, know how far away I am from *agape*. You know that I am only capable of loving you with my imperfect human love: *philia*."

Jesus, however, doesn't back down. He asks a second time, "Do you love (*agapao*) me?" Again, Peter humbly admits he can only love Jesus with his lesser human love: "Lord, you know that I love you (*phileo*)."

---

[1] Pope Benedict XVI, "Peter, the Apostle," General Audience (May 24, 2006).
[2] The word *agape* is the noun related to the verb *agapao*. The word *philia* is the noun related to the verb *phileo*.

Finally, Jesus changes the question. He does not lower the standard of love in any way, but he does lower himself to meet Peter where he is. He accepts what Peter can offer, even if it's only weak, human love. He uses the word *phileo*: "Do you love (*phileo*) me?" Here, Jesus puts himself on Peter's level and does not demand that Peter immediately rise up to his. And that's encouraging to Peter. He replies to Jesus as if to say, "Lord, you know everything. You know this is all I can do on my own. The best I am capable of offering is my weak, human love: *philia*. I wish I could do more, but I humbly entrust this imperfect gift to you."

And here we come to the most amazing part of the story— and the one that sheds light on the drama of our own walk with the Lord. Jesus accepts this imperfect human love of Peter's and transforms it into *agape*. Peter finally presents himself to Jesus as he really is—not in the inflated view he previously had of himself or in the ideal way he'd like to live someday, but in the truth of his own fragility. And once Peter does this, once he comes to terms with the truth about himself—that he is simply not capable of *agape* right now—a new era begins in Peter's friendship with Christ. At precisely this moment, Jesus suddenly starts talking about how Mr. *Philia* Peter will one day live *agape* like Christ himself did. Peter will be changed. His heart will be transformed. One day, Peter will find his hands stretched out on a cross like Jesus's were on Good Friday. Indeed, Jesus foretells Peter's crucifixion in Rome: "'When you are old, you will stretch out your hands, and another will fasten your belt for you and carry you where you do not wish to go' (This he said to show by what death he was to glorify God)" (Jn 21:18–19).

The story of Peter's transformation is the story God wants to write in the hearts of all disciples. Jesus wants to meet us where we are, as we are, with all our fears, wounds, and sins, and transform our *philia* hearts into *agape* hearts. As Pope Benedict XVI once observed,

> From that day, Peter "followed" the Master with the precise awareness of his own fragility; but this understanding did not discourage him. Indeed, he knew that he could count on the presence of the Risen One beside him. From the naïve enthusiasm of initial acceptance, passing through the sorrowful experience of denial and the weeping of conversion, Peter succeeded in entrusting himself to that Jesus who adapted himself to his poor capacity of love. And in this way he shows us the way, notwithstanding all of our weakness. We know that Jesus adapts himself to this weakness of ours. We follow him with our poor capacity to love and we know that Jesus is good and he accepts us.[3]

What Jesus did in Peter he will do in each of us—if we learn to follow him as a disciple.

Being a Disciple

In the first-century world of Jesus, being a disciple was all about one key word: imitation. When a disciple followed a rabbi, he lived with the rabbi, shared meals with the rabbi, prayed with the rabbi, and studied with the rabbi. The goal of the disciple wasn't merely to master his rabbi's teachings, but to imitate the way he lived—the way he prayed, worked, trusted in God's providence, helped the poor, lived friendship, and served the people.

So if we are going to be disciples of Jesus today, we must aim for a lot more than believing a set of doctrines and

---

[3] Pope Benedict XVI, "Peter, the Apostle," General Audience (May 24, 2006). While it is often pointed out that John's Gospel uses *agapao* and *phileo* interchangeably, the play on words in this particular passage, coming as they do in light of Peter's recent failures in love (his threefold denial of Christ), make possible Pope Benedict's pastoral insight and beautiful, spiritual reflection on this scene: Peter humbly recognizing he is incapable of *agapao* and Jesus accepting what Peter can offer.

following the rules of our faith. We must go deeper and consider what's happening interiorly in our spiritual lives: Are we moving closer to Christ, encountering him anew each day and becoming more like him? Do we intentionally strive to live like him, think like him, and love

> Following Jesus as a disciple is a whole way of life—his way of life transforming us.

like him? Being a disciple of Jesus is not about merely going through the motions with our faith—attending Mass, saying some prayers, and avoiding bad things. Following Jesus as a disciple is a whole way of life—*his* way of life transforming us, his *agape* love radiating through our lesser *philia* love.

All of this reminds us that being Catholic is not a stagnant reality ("I identify on this survey as a Catholic.") It's something intensely dynamic. It implies movement and transformation as the disciple deepens his friendship with Christ and becomes ever more like him. Indeed, a disciple humbly recognizes two things:

(A) *The truth about himself*—his many weaknesses, failures, and areas where he falls short of living like Christ

(B) *The truth about what he's made for*—being conformed to the image of Christ: living like him, loving like him, *agapao*

In summary, a true disciple knows what he's made for: transformation in Christ (B). But he also knows the many ways he falls short (A). Discipleship is all about moving from A to B. It's the long journey Peter made from *phileo* to *agapao* that Jesus wants to reproduce in the hearts of all his disciples.

When our Catholic Tradition talks about growing in holiness, pursuing sanctity, and becoming saints, it's basically describing this process of a Christian disciple being conformed to the image of Christ (see Rm 8:29). Most of all, a mature disciple becomes increasingly aware of how this is not something he can do on his own. As with Peter, our discipleship is a lifelong process of becoming ever more convinced of our littleness, learning to rely on God, and cooperating with his grace as we are slowly being transformed into Christ's likeness "from one degree of glory to another" (2 Cor 3:18).

Do you sense that movement in you—that desire to go deeper in your relationship with Christ? Do you have a longing to follow Jesus more closely, to be transformed by him, to move from A to B, from *phileo* to *agapao*? Do you notice a stirring inside, a longing to love God with all your heart, but feel unsure about what steps to take next?

If you answered yes to any of these questions, know that God is the one who has put those yearnings in your soul. He has already given you the heart of a disciple. This book simply aims to help you follow those initial promptings of the Holy Spirit so that you may more intentionally encounter Jesus anew each day and be more disposed to the power of his grace molding you, transforming you ever more into his likeness.

PART ONE

"Be My Disciple"

"Follow Me"

In a small church near the Piazza Navona in Rome, there's a famous painting by the Baroque artist Caravaggio. I like to take pilgrims there, not just to admire the beautiful masterpiece, but for a more important spiritual purpose: to enter into the mystery of what it means to be a disciple.

The painting depicts the gospel account of Jesus inviting Matthew the tax collector to follow him. In Caravaggio's portrayal of this scene, Jesus enters the world of Matthew and his tax collector friends. Light pours through a window behind Jesus and streams into the darkness of the tax collector's hole. The symbolism is clear: Jesus, the Light of the World, is entering the darkness of Matthew's life. He looks Matthew in the eye. He points at Matthew. He calls, "Follow me." What will Matthew do?

Some of Matthew's colleagues next to him don't even notice what's happening. These are men who are too caught up in themselves—unaware of others and oblivious to the fact that Jesus is in their midst. One older man stares at the money on the table, touching his glasses in a miserly way, wondering, "How much money did I make today?" Meanwhile, a youthful tax collector sits at the table forlorn, his head facing downward and his fingers stroking his coins. He has all the money in the world, but he is still empty, unfulfilled, searching for something more. These men are totally unaware of who just entered the room.

But there is one who certainly does notice. It's Matthew. The look on his face tells it all—multiple conflicting emotions torment him all at once. On one hand, Matthew is completely shocked that Jesus is pointing at him: "You want me, a tax collector, a sinner, to follow you? You've got to be kidding! You must be thinking of someone else!"

On the other hand, Matthew's expression suggests there's a part of him that's actually considering the new possibility: "I wonder what it would be like to follow this Jesus? What would my life be like if I made this change?...Maybe my life would be better. Maybe I'd be happier. I wonder if I should do this?"

But, in the same instant, Matthew also has a look of terror on his face—frightened over the mere thought of such a dramatic life change. "There's no way I could do that! I don't want to leave my job, my career, my reputation, my friends....I don't want to let go of my money bags!"

Caravaggio's painting beautifully captures Matthew at the point of decision—that pivotal moment between Matthew the tax collector and Matthew the disciple. What will Matthew do?

Holding On to Our Money Bags

Maybe you've been there before. Maybe you've experienced certain moments when you sense God is calling you to do something. It may not be an extraordinary spiritual experience, like seeing visions or having angels appear to you. Just a subtle sense that you're supposed to do something or not do something. You wonder if you should make a small change (call your mom, give extra attention to one of your children, visit a friend, or join a Bible study at your parish). You sense you need to say you're sorry to your spouse for something. You're frustrated by someone's actions but suddenly realize you should respond with patience. You ponder whether you're spending too much time at work and not enough time with your family.

> Jesus knocks on the door of our hearts. Will we let him in?

Those little nudges from God, those subtle promptings of the Holy Spirit, are moments when Jesus is inviting you to follow him more closely. And they happen often in the midst of ordinary Christians' daily lives. They may not be as dramatic as that occasion when Jesus walked into Matthew's tax collector's office, but the point is identical. The same Jesus, the Light of the World, knocks on the door of our hearts. He wants to enter our lives and shine his light on any areas of darkness that keep us from a closer relationship with him. Will we let him in?

Caravaggio's painting invites us to do just that: to welcome Jesus into our lives more, to put ourselves in Matthew's shoes and experience anew Jesus's call to follow him more closely as disciples.

Me, a Disciple?

Unfortunately, many Christians don't view themselves as disciples. "I'm just a normal Christian. I go to church. I believe. I try to be a good person. But I'm not good enough to be a disciple." Too often, we view "ordinary Christians" and "disciples" as being in two separate categories. Disciples are those super-Christians, those who are part of an elite group of religious leaders or exceptionally spiritual people. Bishops, priests, Mother Teresa, lay leaders, and those "very religious" people who show up at every event at my parish—those are disciples. "But I'm just an ordinary guy in Pew Number 16. I could never be a disciple."

But what if I were to tell you that being a disciple is not beyond you and that it's something you've probably already begun experiencing in your relationship with God? What if I were to tell you that learning how to live more intentionally as a disciple can make all the difference in your spiritual life?

If you desire a closer, more intimate relationship with Jesus—if you desire your spiritual life to grow more profoundly and go far beyond the humdrum existence of a Christian who is just going through the motions—then step back with me and consider what it means to follow Jesus intentionally as a *disciple*.

Reflection Questions

- Put yourself in the scene where Jesus calls St. Matthew. If Jesus walked into the room and pointed to you, saying, "Follow me," what would you be thinking? How would you respond to his call?

- In that moment, St. Matthew was probably tempted to cling to his money bags. What keeps you from following Christ more fully? What "money bags" might Jesus be asking you to let go of?

Total Commitment

Are you a true *follower* of Jesus or just a *fan*?

Jesus never had problems attracting people to his ministry. Word about his movement spread quickly and large crowds from throughout the region came out to see him. They were impressed by his dynamic teaching, which made him stand out from other teachers of his day: This man teaches "as one who [has] authority, and not as the scribes" (Mk 1:22). They also were intrigued by his many healings and miracles: "We never saw anything like this!" (Mk 2:12). They even saw him as a great leader—a prophet and the long-awaited Messiah-King (see Jn 6:14–15)— someone they could rally around in the hopes that he would give them a better life.

So Jesus had high approval ratings for much of his public ministry. He had many *fans*. But he was looking for more than that. He was looking for souls who would follow him completely, as disciples.

And the same is true today.

There are many of us who wear various Catholic "badges"—perhaps we attend Catholic conferences, show up at parish events, say certain prayers, enjoy fellowship with other like-minded believers, listen to Catholic radio, and vote for the "right" political candidate. From all outward appearances, we seem to be very interested in Catholic things. But inside, are we truly committed to the Lord? Have we surrendered our lives to Christ, seeking to fulfill *his* plan for our lives and not our own?

In other words, are we merely fans of Jesus or true followers? As in his own day, Jesus now is looking for souls who are willing to do more than the crowds who are fascinated by all things Catholic. He's looking for those who are willing to do what he wants them to do, say what he wants them to say, go where he wants them to go, and give up whatever he wants them to give up. That's a lot more than being a fan. In other words, Jesus is looking for souls willing to give a total commitment to him as disciples.

Not Just a Part of Our Lives, but the Center

Following Jesus as a disciple represents a decisive turning point in a person's life—a major break with the past and a complete reordering of priorities, which now will be centered on the Person of Jesus Christ. Things we used to think were really important—money, success, comfort, possessions, reputation, dreams for our kids, certain relationships we thought would fulfill us—are now seen through the lens of Jesus. This doesn't necessarily mean we must give up all our dreams, hopes, possessions, and enjoyments of this world. But we must put our relationship with Jesus above all these things.

Here's the key: Jesus doesn't just want to be a part of our lives; he wants to be at the very *center*. He wants to be the number one thing in our lives. "Seek first his kingdom" (Mt 6:33). And if we do that—if we truly put Jesus first above everything else in our lives—then we find that all those other desires, dreams, and concerns will sort themselves out. "Seek first his kingdom and his righteousness, *and all these things shall be yours as well*" (Mt 6:33, emphasis added). For God's plans are bigger than our own. He knows what's best for us, and he wants us to be happy more than we do. Will we entrust our lives to him? Will we seek his plan for our lives? Or will we cling to our control and only surrender certain parts of our lives to him?

Where Is Your Treasure?

For me, a critical turning point in my faith came in my young adult years. I was raised Catholic and had never left the Church. I went to Mass each week and was involved in my parish probably more than most young adults were. I wanted to grow in my faith and even participated in some Catholic activities that helped me do that. *I was a part of the crowd*—believing in God and practicing my faith, but not yet surrendering my life to him.

In those years, Jesus was truly a part of my life. But, if I had to be honest, he wasn't at the center. There were many other things that competed for my attention and won: getting good grades, getting a good job, success, having a girlfriend, having fun. And while there was nothing wrong with pursuing any of those things, they became more important to me than

> Jesus doesn't just want to be a part of our lives; he wants to be at the very *center*.

my relationship with God. I treasured those things more. And that tells you something about my heart at that time. "For where your treasure is, there will your heart be also" (Mt 6:21).

But God used two pivotal moments in those years to turn my life around and bring me closer to him.

Are You Happy?

First, a friend once asked me a very simple question when we were out for coffee catching up: "So, are you happy?"

No one had ever asked me that question before. It made me a little uncomfortable because it challenged me to look inside more than I was used to. I nervously replied, "Happy? Uh...well...I guess so. Yeah, I'm happy."

My friend just sat and listened. He said nothing, letting the silence linger, waiting to see if I would say anything more. I felt more uncomfortable and said, "Oh sure, I'm happy.... I've got good grades. I won an internship. Our band is playing well together. I've got a girlfriend....Yeah, I'm happy."

But I left that conversation rattled. Unsettled. For weeks, his simple question haunted me: "*Are you happy?*" I slowly began to realize that, deep down, I wasn't really happy. Yes, on the outside it looked as if I had it all—everything the world would want. But on the inside, I was empty, searching for something more. I had certain fears, insecurities, and worries about where my life was going. I definitely wasn't satisfied with my life. Looking back, I could say with the great St. Augustine that my heart was restless because it did not rest in God.[1]

Surrender

That conversation paved the way for a turning point experience that would come some time later. I went on a weekend retreat with some other young adults. At the climax of the retreat on Saturday night, a priest gave a reflection on

---

[1] St. Augustine, *Confessions*, trans. R.S. Pine-Coffin (New York: Penguin Books, 1961), 1, 1, 1.

the Gospel story about the rich young man. I had heard the story before, but never spelled out quite like this.

The priest pointed out how impressive this young man was. He wanted a good relationship with God. He even approached Jesus, asking him what he needed to do to inherit eternal life. Jesus told him to follow the commandments, and the man responded he did that already. What an impressive young man! How many people can say they follow all the commandments?

But the young man didn't stop there. He wanted to do more for God, and he asked Jesus what else he should do. Think about that: This obedient, law-abiding Jewish man wanted to do whatever he could to follow God. What a good heart. Jesus, however, pointed out one thing he still lacked. Jesus challenged him to be willing to give up everything and follow him.

> For weeks, his simple question haunted me: *"Are you happy?"*

At that, however, the young man held back. He loved God and wanted to follow Jesus, but he could not take that most crucial step of faith—saying yes to Jesus, surrendering his life to Christ, giving up everything, putting Jesus first, and following him. Instead, he turned away sad.

I had never heard this scene drawn out so much as I did that night. And I had never felt so personally right in the middle of a biblical story. In the chapel that night, I realized I was that young man—I did the right things, said the right things, acted in the right way, and sincerely wanted to follow God, but I was unwilling to entrust my entire life into Jesus's hands and put him first in my life as Lord.

I stayed in the chapel late that night. Long after everyone else left and went to bed, I knew what I needed to do. I got on my knees and told Jesus I didn't want to be the rich young man. I didn't want to walk away sad. I wanted to give my life to him. I wanted to follow him fully, not just in part. I wanted to surrender my life to him unconditionally and seek his will, not my own. I didn't use the biblical language we have been discussing in this book, but the point was the same. I was basically telling Jesus I wanted to follow him unconditionally *as a disciple*.

Take, Lord, and Receive . . .

Have you ever said a prayer like that before—a prayer of surrender, placing your entire life in God's hands? It's a wonderful thing to do, something many saints have done in different ways. And even if we have said a similar prayer in the past, it's still a good thing to renew this commitment to Christ regularly.

Too often, the best of us easily fall back into old habits. We forget that God is really in charge. We get too caught up in our own busyness and pursuits. When I wake up in the morning, do I think about what I want to do today, or do I ask the Lord how he wants to use my life to serve him, my spouse, my friends, and my community? In other words, do I fall into doing what I want with my life—using my life for my purposes? Or do I sincerely seek first the Kingdom and pursue what Christ wants—using my life for his purposes and not my own?

One great prayer from the Catholic tradition that helps us welcome Christ's lordship in our lives comes from St. Ignatius of Loyola. Whether you have recited a prayer of surrender long ago or are doing it for the first time, you can pause now and maybe even kneel down to pray with these beautiful words of St. Ignatius that help us entrust our lives to Jesus, putting his plan for our lives before our own.

Take, Lord, and receive all my liberty,
my memory, my understanding, and my entire will,
all that I have and possess.
Thou hast given all to me.
To Thee, O Lord, I return it.
All is Thine; dispose of it wholly according to Thy will.
Give me Thy love and Thy grace,
for this is sufficient for me.[2]

Seek First the Kingdom

When we truly welcome Jesus as Lord of our lives, we experience a great mystery. It's the mystery of self-giving. When I give up control over my life—my plans, my hopes, my desires—and entrust it all into the hands of God, when I follow his moral teachings and live according to the way he made me, I actually discover fullness of life at a deeper level because I'm surrendering my life to God's plan, which is so much greater than my own.

That's what happened to countless other Christians who have committed their lives to Christ. Their lives are changed. There's a deeper peace, joy, and sense of purpose that comes when we live for Christ and not for ourselves. Problems don't go away. Suffering still exists. We still face many challenges. But we see those trials now as crosses and not as random occasions of suffering or "bad luck." And we realize we are not alone. Jesus is truly there to help us through them.

Looking back on that conversation over coffee, I'm so grateful for my friend's question. If he asked me today "Are

---

[2] St. Ignatius of Loyola, *Spiritual Exercises*, trans. Louis J. Puhl, SJ (Chicago: Loyola University Press, 1951), 102.

you happy?" there would be no hesitation or awkwardness. I'd give a wholehearted "Yes!" That doesn't mean I've got it all figured out now. I'm still very much a work in progress and have a long way to go in my discipleship. And I experience times of sorrow, frustration, and disappointment like every human being does. But my fundamental identity in Christ has made one thing clear: with Jesus as Lord of my life, I have experienced deep, lasting joy, peace, and purpose I never had before.

But what does it mean to follow Jesus in this way? What does it look like to have Jesus not just as a part of your life but as the very center of your life, to be not just a fan but a true follower? To get a picture of what to do and what to aim for in your relationship with Jesus, let's turn now to God's Word in Scripture and discover what God himself teaches about the life of a disciple.

Reflection Questions

- Which of the following best describes your relationship with Jesus?

    - Jesus is on the outside of my life. Not important to me at all.

    - Jesus is a part of my life. Important, but honestly just one of many things.

    - Jesus is at the very center of my life. The most important part and motivation for all I do.

- Do you want a closer friendship with Christ? If so, what would it take to have him more at the center?

- Consider the "Take, Lord, and Receive..." prayer from St. Ignatius of Loyola quoted in this chapter. What part of this prayer of surrender is most challenging for you? Why? Ask Jesus for the grace to help you sincerely desire what this prayer expresses.

In the Dust of the Rabbi

So you want to follow Jesus as a disciple. But what does that mean? What does that look like? To shed light on this, I want to take you back in time to the first-century Jewish world in which Jesus lived to consider what it meant for a disciple to follow a rabbi.

If there's one key word that sums up the essence of discipleship, it's *imitation*—imitating the life of the teacher. Though the word *disciple* (*mathetes*) means "learner," a Jewish disciple gained more from his rabbi than just book knowledge. Discipleship was more of an apprenticeship—an immersion into the rabbi's whole way of life. A disciple would live with the rabbi, share meals with the rabbi, pray with the rabbi, and observe the way the rabbi studied, taught, rested, served the poor, interacted with his friends, and debated other teachers. And the goal of discipleship was to emulate the master's entire way of living. Jesus sums up this point, saying, "Every one when he is fully taught will be like his teacher" (Lk 6:40).

Thus, when Jesus commissions his Apostles to take the Gospel to the ends of the earth, he tells them not just to spread information but to "go therefore and make *disciples* of all nations," teaching them to "observe" all that he has commanded them (Mt 28:19–20, emphasis added). Notice the emphasis is not merely on head knowledge. While disciples certainly need to know the *content* of his message, Jesus stresses the importance of *observing* his teachings, putting them into practice in their daily lives. *Living out* the teachings was more important than merely *knowing* them.

Similarly, the Apostle Paul teaches that the goal of the Christian life is not just *believing* the truths Jesus reveals but *imitating* the Lord Jesus. The followers of Jesus, he says, are made "to be conformed to the image of his Son" (Rm 8:29). When Paul raises up disciples of his own, he emphasizes the importance not just of learning concepts from him but also of imitation: "Be imitators of me, as I am of Christ" (1 Cor 11:1). When he sends his own disciples to form others, Paul's message is still focused on imitation: "I urge you, then, be imitators of me. Therefore I sent to you Timothy, my beloved and faithful child in the Lord, to remind you of my ways in Christ, as I teach them everywhere in every church" (1 Cor 4:16–17).

> When Christians talk about "growing in holiness," they are, in essence, talking about discipleship.

This biblical notion of discipleship beautifully expresses what the Christian life is all about: the imitation of Christ. It is the lifelong process of encountering Jesus anew each day, like Matthew does that moment in the tax collector's office, and being changed by Jesus so that we become more like him. But this encounter is not a one-time act. Jesus is constantly calling us to take that next step in faith, that next step closer to him. Indeed, he calls us throughout our lives to *ongoing* conversion so that we become more like Christ. Over time, we start to think as he thinks, see as he sees, love as he loves, and act as he acts. When Christians talk about "growing in holiness" or "pursuing sanctity" or "becoming saints," they are, in essence, talking about the *imitatio Christi*, or what the Scriptures would call discipleship.

Apprenticeship

In biblical times, following someone as his disciple was very different from modern classroom learning. On a college campus, a professor might give lectures to students in a large hall; the students take notes, and they're examined on the material later in the semester. But there's usually not an ongoing personal relationship and sharing of daily life between professor and student in the university setting today.

To follow a rabbi, however, meant living with the rabbi, sharing life with him, and taking part in the rabbi's whole way of life. A disciple might accompany a rabbi on all his daily routines: prayer, study, debating other rabbis, giving alms to the poor, burying the dead, going to court, etc. A rabbi's life was meant to be a living example of someone shaped by God's Word. Disciples, therefore, studied not just the text of Scripture but also the "text" of the rabbi's life.

I experienced a discipleship-like apprenticeship in my young adult years when I was blessed to live for almost three months with a well-known saintly Jesuit theologian named Father John Hardon, SJ. A leading teacher of the Faith who published many books on prayer, the Sacraments, and the teachings of the Church, Father Hardon stood out to many in his era as a hero, explaining and defending the Catholic Faith in an age of much doctrinal and moral confusion. I happened to have a few months free while I was transitioning between my career in the corporate world and my graduate studies in theology. The idea of living with and working alongside Father Hardon for three months seemed like a great opportunity for me to learn theology from one of the master teachers of the day.

But God had other plans.

Don't get me wrong. I did gain some important theological foundations from my time with Father Hardon. But the most profound lessons I learned from him—the ones that have stuck with me the most and helped shape who I have become—were not about doctrines. They were about his way of life.

I noticed, for example, the way he prayed. Each day he rose before dawn for prayer in the chapel and then celebrated Mass. He also seemed to pray unceasingly throughout the day. In between meetings. Walking from the cafeteria to his office. Going from his room to my car. Driving from one place to the next. Waiting in the doctor's office. He saw these "in-between" times as opportunities for him to love Jesus. He was very ordinary and human, and in these moments, he would talk to people about their days, their families, the Michigan game on Saturday. But he also filled these little spaces with gifts of love to God, offering Our Fathers, *Memorares*, or decades of the Rosary.

I also was moved by his ardent devotion to the Eucharist. He always seemed to be going to the Blessed Sacrament, making many brief visits to the chapel throughout the day. Whenever walking from one part of the building to the other, he would want to pass the chapel, even if it wasn't the most direct route. He always stopped in, just for a quick minute. He'd enter the chapel, genuflect, make the Sign of the Cross, and look at the Tabernacle as if he were in conversation with a good friend. And whenever he faced some problem or difficulty, he would make a beeline straight to Jesus in the Eucharist, instinctively taking his troubles immediately to the Lord.

I also noticed how he studied and prepared for his classes. He didn't spend much time in his office. Almost all of his work was done in the chapel with Jesus in the Eucharist. He would bring a book and some paper and write the outlines for his classes often before the Blessed Sacrament. He would read a few lines, write a few lines, look up at the Tabernacle, talk to Jesus about what he was reading and teaching, and then write a little more.

And I remember the way he dealt with suffering—always remaining joyful and focused on others. When I was with him, he was already quite elderly and in a lot of physical pain. In fact, on the day I arrived, he had had cataract surgery that morning. I remember him coming into the building with one eye patched, moving very slowly, clearly in a lot of pain. But he still smiled, shook my hand, and with sincere joy said, "Welcome!...It is so good you are here." I remember thinking, "Are you kidding me? It's so good that *you* are here!" Yet that was Father Hardon—never caught up in his own troubles, always focused on Jesus and on others.

Many other aspects of his life stood out to me: his love of going to Confession, his total abandonment to Divine Providence for every event in his life, his patience and gentleness with parish leaders who opposed Church teaching, his compassion for those who were suffering. Perhaps most moving was his radiant love for Jesus. Whenever he spoke the name of Jesus, he clearly wasn't talking about someone who lived a long time ago or some God out there in the universe. This was a man who truly knew Jesus, personally, intimately, right now. When he said "Jesus," it was like a lover tenderly speaking the name of his beloved.

All this left quite an impression on me—much more than any textbook or classroom lecture could. Indeed, Father Hardon never sat me down and said, "Here are seven important lessons you need to learn about the life of a theologian." But because I was sharing life with him day in and day out, some of his habits thankfully rubbed off on me a little. As a saying goes, "More is caught than taught." While I can only hope to be as prayerful, holy, and compassionate as Father Hardon, I am grateful for how his example has impacted my life. When I find myself stopping by the chapel at different points throughout the day or filling "in-between" times with short prayers, for example, I know that idea didn't come from me. It came from his example. Or if I catch myself being patient and kind with those who hold misguided theological positions, I know that gentle approach wasn't something I came up with on my own. I learned it from watching him be that way again and again. Even the section of the book you're reading right now was written in the Eucharistic chapel as I was talking to Jesus about it. Thank you, Father Hardon! And thank you, Jesus, for bringing Father Hardon into my life.

"Come and See"

I only had three months with Father Hardon. Imagine spending three years not just with a wise, holy teacher like him, but with the Son of God himself! That's what the original disciples of Jesus are given the chance to do. Jesus invites these men not just to attend his public lectures, but to live with him, share meals with him, pray with him, teach with him, serve the poor with him, and share life with him.

Indeed, this is the kind of apprenticeship the first disciples are seeking from Jesus when they ask him, "Where are you staying?" (Jn 1:38). With this question, they are not inquiring about Jesus's lodging preferences. They are subtly expressing their desire *to stay with Jesus as a disciple stays with a rabbi*. Similarly, when Jesus replies, "Come and see" (Jn 1:39), he isn't asking them to come check out his digs. He is inviting them to discipleship.

This invitation marks the beginning of a life-shaping training for them. They will never be the same. It is as if Jesus were inviting them to join him on a three-year camping trip as they journey from one village to the next throughout Galilee during his itinerant public ministry. (And you really get to know people when you go camping with them!) When Jesus tells the disciples, "Follow me" (Jn 1:43), he means that not just in the spatial sense

> If you encounter a rabbi, you should "cover yourself in the dust of his feet and drink in his words thirstily."
> —Rabbinic saying

of accompanying him in his ministry from one point to another. He means it in the sense of spiritually walking in his footsteps, imitating his entire way of living—in other words, following him as a disciple.

Over the course of many weeks and months, the disciples absorb much from Jesus's way of living. They notice the way he wakes up early to pray and the time he has in solitude with God. They witness his compassion in helping the sick, the blind, the lepers, and others who are suffering. They are struck by his pressing need to go out to the peripheries, to those who are sinners, Gentiles, or social outcasts, and invite them into his Kingdom. They also observe the way Jesus debates his opponents, the way he teaches the crowds, how he calls people to repent, and how he offers them love and mercy. Over time, they begin to absorb this way of life.

According to one ancient Jewish saying, if you encounter a rabbi, you should "cover yourself in the dust of his feet and drink in his words thirstily."[1] The expression probably draws on a well-known sight for ancient Jews: disciples were known for walking behind their rabbi, following him so closely that they would become covered with the dust kicked up from his sandals. This would have been a powerful image for what should happen in the disciple's life spiritually. Disciples were expected to follow their rabbi so closely that they would be covered with their master's whole way of thinking, living, and acting.

And if we wish to follow Jesus as disciples, we will do the same. Even though Jesus lived 2,000 years ago, he is still alive today, and we can encounter him personally—in prayer, in the Sacraments, in fellowship with others, and in learning about what he taught and how he lived. Through these practices (which we will discuss in Part Three), we can encounter Jesus anew and his life can "rub off" on us. Over time, we will be transformed little by little, taking on the character of Christ, imitating his way of life.

But to do that, we must do a lot more than just be Christians who show up at Mass and go through the motions with our faith. We must truly strive to imitate Christ Jesus, seeking to be covered with the dust of our good Rabbi. How practically to do that is what we consider next.

---

[1]   Mishnah, *Pirkei Avot* 1:4.

Reflection Questions

- How does the idea of discipleship as an apprenticeship, an imitation of the Master, change the way you view your life as a Christian? What is most inspiring about it? What is most intimidating?

- What is one aspect of Christ's life you'd like to imitate more in your life now? What can you do practically this week to live more like Christ in this area?

The Struggle

How do I know I'm following Jesus faithfully as a disciple? I go to Mass. I say some prayers. I volunteer at my parish and try to be a good person. Is that enough?

My wife and I once left our cheerful, bubbly five-year-old daughter with a babysitter who was watching her and her friends for an afternoon. The babysitter later reported an interesting incident that sheds light on a key quality that makes someone a disciple and not just a Christian going through the motions with his or her faith.

The children were wrestling and dog-piling on top of each other. The babysitter gently told our daughter to be careful and not to be so rough. As soon as she heard her name called, however, our daughter immediately jumped out of the pile of kids and stood up straight like a soldier with a very serious, sad look on her face. She stood there in silence as if she were awaiting some instructions from the captain.

The babysitter was puzzled by this response and asked her, "What's wrong?"

With an anguished expression, she replied sorrowfully, "Ohhhhh...I've been *trying* to be good!"

The babysitter smiled and asked, "How's that been going for you?"

With tears now streaming down her face, my daughter said, "It's really, really hard!"

"Trying to be good" is hard not just for little children, but also for us adult children of God, isn't it? We *want* to be good Christians. We *want* to be more thoughtful with our spouses, more patient with our kids, more generous with our neighbors, more faithful to our time in prayer. But we struggle. We fall short. We don't improve at the pace we'd like.

From time to time, we might even sense God nudging us— inviting us to love more, to give more, to trust more, to serve more, to surrender more in some particular way. When we get those moments of inspiration, we might be filled with joy, peace, and even enthusiasm about the new direction we want to take. But if we're honest,

> Jesus shines his light on the dark corners of our souls.

we must admit that sometimes there's another part of us that's not so excited. We're afraid. We hesitate. We hold back. We're not sure we want to change. We cling to our money bags as Matthew was tempted to do.

This is the drama of discipleship. Do you have that inner struggle? Are you really striving to live more like Christ—are you earnestly "*trying* to be good"? Or are you just going through the motions with your faith, muddling through life, avoiding bad things but not striving for greatness?

Jesus draws near to those whom he loves. He presses in and wants to change us. He wants to do with us what he did with Matthew: shine his light on the dark corners of our souls and invite us to follow him more closely. Sometimes, we're inspired by his invitation. Other times, we're terrified by it. Most of the time, we experience a mixture of both. Do you experience this pull and tug, this interior struggle, in your relationship with God? Are you intentionally seeking

to root out bad habits and sins in your life and take on the
qualities of Christ? Are you willing to draw nearer to God
and allow him to change you? If you are, these are some key
signs that you are on the path of discipleship.

Many saints, martyrs, and leaders have described this
inner battle not just theoretically, but personally, as taking
place in their own souls. Pope Francis, for example, when
he was archbishop of Buenos Aires, would come to Rome
for meetings in the Vatican and often visit the church where
Caravaggio's painting *The Calling of St. Matthew* resides. He
would go to that same side chapel to pray and contemplate
the scene. Pope Francis himself relates that he often senses
God calling him to greater love, patience, and generosity,
but he often feels like Matthew at this moment. A part of
him wants to say yes and give more and surrender more,
while another part of him wants to remain in his comfort
zone and not have to change.

> That finger of Jesus, pointing at Matthew. That's me. I feel like him.
> Like Matthew.... It is the gesture of Matthew that strikes me: he holds
> on to his money as if to say, "No, not me! No, this money is mine."
> Here, this is me, a sinner on whom the Lord has turned his gaze.[1]

Both Caravaggio and Pope Francis are describing, in paint
and words respectively, what goes on inside countless
ordinary Christians throughout the world: the struggle of a
true disciple.

Chicago Cubs Catholics

In the foundational document of his pontificate, *The Joy of the
Gospel*, Pope Francis calls on all Christians to renew their daily

---

[1]   Anthony Spadaro, "A Big Heart Open to God: The Exclusive Interview with
Pope Francis," *America* magazine, September 30, 2013.

encounter with Jesus *as disciples*. After noting how many within the Church fall prey to the self-centered attitudes prevalent in our modern world—attitudes that hinder our ability to follow Jesus—he exhorts us to turn to the one thing that can make all the difference for living our faith in a secular age: interior renewal in Christ. "I invite all Christians, everywhere, at this very moment, to a renewed personal encounter with Jesus Christ, or at least an openness to letting him encounter them; I ask all of you to do this unfailingly each day."[2]

This is quite remarkable. The pope seems concerned that there are many Christians who do not regularly encounter Jesus in a personal relationship. Outwardly, we might say and do the right things. We show up at Mass. We put money in the collection basket. We say a prayer before meals. We go to a parish event every once in a while. We might even sing in the choir, attend a Bible study, or serve as a Eucharistic minister. All this is good, but *inwardly*, do we regularly encounter Our Lord Jesus who is calling us to take that next step of faith and inviting us into a deeper relationship with him? In other words, Pope Francis is challenging us to consider whether we are living as disciples who strive to imitate the Master or as people who are going through the motions with our faith.

Or I might put it this way: Are we striving for a deeper union with God and greatness in our spiritual lives? Or are we just Chicago Cubs Catholics?

For 108 years, my dear Chicago Cubs were the epitome of mediocrity. Yes, they finally won the World Series in 2016, but from 1908 to 2015 they were known as the beloved losers. As

---

[2]   Pope Francis, apostolic exhortation *Evangelii gaudium* (The Joy of the Gospel) (November 24, 2013), no. 3.

Cubs fans, every June we'd start saying the same three words: "Maybe next year." If we happened to end a season at .500 we'd feel pretty good about ourselves. "Wow, we won half our games this year. Not bad!" And if we made the playoffs once every decade or so, that was quite the accomplishment. But the World Series? For the Cubs? No. That was only for the really good teams in Major League Baseball!

We Christians can sometimes adopt a similar attitude. If we believe in God, show up to Mass each week, give up something for Lent, try to be good to others, and maybe even volunteer for something at the parish, we feel pretty good about ourselves. We tell ourselves, "I go to church. I'm nice to people. I don't murder or rob banks. I'm doing okay as a Christian." But to strive to be a *great* Catholic? "No, that's not for me. That's only for the really holy people like Mother Teresa and the pope!"

Orthodoxy as an Excuse

Another obstacle to following Jesus as a disciple is placing too much emphasis on different aspects of our Faith. Some of us, for example, might turn to orthodoxy as the sole measure for being a good Catholic. "I believe in the Sacraments. I'm pro-life. I defend marriage. I follow the pope and believe all the Church's teachings." Especially in an era when many Catholics don't know, doubt, or even reject Church teaching, we might be tempted to pat ourselves on the back and congratulate ourselves for our solid Catholic convictions. "Well, I'm doing better than most. Many people today don't even believe in God. And most baptized Catholics don't go to Mass every Sunday. I at least do that. Also, so many other Christians in the world are wavering on crucial moral issues today like abortion, contraception, the definition of marriage, and care for the poor. But I remain faithful to the Church's teachings, so I'm doing better than most. God must be very pleased with me."

Let me be clear. Believing the right things (the word *orthodoxy* means "right doctrine") is absolutely essential. We must follow the teachings of Jesus as passed on through the Church. But it's not enough. It's just the basic starting point for any disciple of Jesus. Remember, discipleship is about imitating the Master, not just getting the right answers on a theology quiz. The heart of the matter is not only believing the right things, but also living as Jesus lived.

Imagine if I told you I was a great basketball player and you asked me what makes me so good on the court. What would you think if I said, "I'm a great basketball player because I follow all the rules. I think following the rules is important. I stay inbounds. I don't double dribble. I don't travel with the ball. I'm an awesome basketball player!" Certainly, following the rules is essential, but that's just permission to play. That doesn't make me the next Michael Jordan! If I follow all the rules but don't have the ability to dribble, shoot, pass, rebound, defend, and block, then I'm simply not a good basketball player.

Similarly, if I believe all the right things and follow all the right rules, that alone doesn't make me a great Catholic. The heart of the matter is my interior struggle to imitate Christ in my daily life. If I believe all the right things but don't grow in prayer, kindness, purity, patience, mercy, forgiveness, generosity, and care for the weak and the poor, I am failing in my life as a disciple. Without love, all the outward badges of faith do not render me a faithful disciple. "If I speak in tongues of men and of angels, but have not love, I am a noisy gong or a clanging cymbal. And if I have prophetic powers, and understand all mysteries and all knowledge, and if I have all faith, so as to remove mountains, but have not love, I am nothing. If I give away all I have, and if I deliver my body to be burned, but have not love, I gain nothing" (1 Cor 13:1–3).

I'm sure God is appreciative of our orthodoxy, but we must remember that that's not what makes anyone a great disciple. It's just the bare minimum, "permission to play," a basic starting point for living the Catholic life.

So if you long to do more than just believe the right things and follow the rules—if you long to do more than just go through the motions with your faith; indeed, if you long to love Jesus "with all your heart, and with all your soul, and with all your might" (Dt 6:5)—then let's take a closer look at the heart of discipleship.

Reflection Questions

- What's the difference between a Christian who follows all the rules and one who lives as a disciple? How do you tend to view your life as a Christian—more oriented toward rule-following or discipleship? What can you do to live more on the discipleship end of this spectrum?

- We all have weaknesses. But how much are you earnestly striving to overcome your weaknesses and live more like Christ? Is there an area of your life right now that you know needs improvement, but you haven't put enough effort into that spiritual battle? What's something you can do this week to give God your best in this struggle?

Not Perfect, but Chosen

We've learned how rabbi-disciple relationships in ancient Judaism can shed light on Christian discipleship. Now it's time to turn to some differences and distinctive features of what Jesus asks of his disciples. And these can be just as enlightening for what they tell us about our walk with the Lord today.

Here are five key points to consider:

1. Jesus is not chosen by his disciples. He chooses them.

2. Jesus is not just a teacher. He is Lord.

3. Jesus's disciples are not models of perfection. They are models of a process.

4. Jesus is not only a role model to imitate. He abides in us, changing us from within.

5. Jesus does not call us to comfort. He calls us to "take up [the] cross" (Mt 16:24).

Each of these differences sheds important light on our relationship with Jesus.

First, You Are Chosen.

"You did not choose me, but I chose you" (Jn 15:16).

That statement from Jesus would have stood out in the Judaism of his day. Back then, it was common for men to consider various rabbis and then choose the master under whom they wanted to be taught. But with Jesus things are markedly different. A person becomes a disciple when called by Jesus himself. Jesus is the one who takes the initiative. He calls individuals to follow him and those who accept this invitation become his disciples.

We see this especially in his public ministry, which is launched after John the Baptist is arrested. He sees Peter and Andrew fishing on the Sea of Galilee and calls them, saying, "Follow me and I will make you become fishers of men" (Mk 1:17). He similarly sees James and John in a boat tending their nets and calls them as well (see Mk 1:19–20). He even invites the tax collector Matthew to become a disciple, saying to him what he said to the others: "Follow me" (Mk 2:14). In each of these cases, Jesus takes the initiative. He seeks the person out. He chooses him.

When others take the initiative, however, it usually doesn't go so well. Several approach Jesus expressing a desire to follow him, but those attempts fail. A scribe, for example, says he'll follow Jesus wherever he goes. But does he really mean it? The man seems to be working off the common model of men seeking to enlist themselves to study under the most well-known or best equipped rabbi. But Jesus checks the scribe's enthusiasm, underscoring how discipleship with him will be different. Jesus has no synagogue or school. Nor is he part of the religious establishment or in a prestigious position in society. He doesn't even have a place to lay his head (see Lk 9:57–58).

Other men tell Jesus they want to follow him but their family ties hold them back (see Mt 8:21–22; Lk 9:61–62).

And when a rich young man turns to Jesus seeking his guidance as a wise teacher, Jesus invites him to discipleship, but he turns away sadly because he's too attached to his possessions (see Mk 10:17–27). In each of these cases, the individuals are intrigued by Jesus. They clearly respect him and, at least in part, sincerely want to follow him. But their interest in discipleship comes with some parameters. They are unwilling to follow Jesus unconditionally, and so none of them end up becoming true disciples.

> We say we want to follow Jesus, but we set up all sorts of limits around how much we're willing to do.

Here's the problem: When we take the initiative and choose Jesus, we tend to do so on our own terms, with many conditions. We say we want to follow Jesus but we set up all sorts of limits around how much we're willing to do. We're afraid of giving up control. We're afraid that we'll miss out on something we want—or that he'll take something away from us.

But if we reflect on the fact that God took the initiative and that he lovingly chose us first, it helps break down our walls of fear and control. When we see that he, out of love, took the first step toward us and chose us for a mission only we can fulfill, we can move forward in confidence, entrusting ourselves more to him, to the mission put into our hands and to all the wonderful blessings he has in store for us.

Never Alone

This realization has dramatic implications for how we see our own lives as disciples. Long before we chose to follow Jesus, he already chose us. Even in times when we weren't making God the top priority, he was ardently pursuing us, putting certain people, events, conversations, and situations in our lives to draw us closer and closer to him. Our becoming disciples was not our work, but the Lord's.

Think about your own faith journey. What brought you to a deeper, more committed faith? Whom did God put in your life to inspire you to follow him more closely? Was there a certain family member, priest, friend, or group of Christians whose example or encouragement helped you grow in your relationship with God? Were there certain events or circumstances in your life that helped you realize your need to make God more of a priority?

Realize that these were not random people, events, and circumstances. The God who loves you was seeking you out, putting these people in your life, and allowing you to face certain situations to bring you closer to him. Your deepened faith life is not of your own initiative. Long before you turned to God, he was running after you. *You were chosen.*

And we can trust that the same Jesus who brought us to the point of conversion and Christian commitment—the same Jesus who loves us so much he did not want us to be distant from him—will continue to seek us out and draw us ever closer to him. He told his disciples, "I am with you always, to the close of the age" (Mt 28:20). So we are never alone. Our following Jesus is not our own work. It's not entirely up to us. We were chosen. The Jesus who chose us to be his disciples wants to complete the work he has begun in us more than we do.

Second, Jesus Is No Ordinary Rabbi. He's God!

Jesus doesn't just claim to be a good teacher, someone who expounds on the Jewish Scriptures and exhorts people to be more loving, forgiving, and faithful to God's law. Jesus does so much more than this. *He claims to be God*—the God who became man and took on human flesh. If we read the Gospels in their first-century Jewish context, it's clear that Jesus is acting and speaking in the Person of God, which is something no other Jewish rabbi ever dared to do.

Take, for example, Jesus's forgiving other people's sins. From the biblical Jewish mindset, this was something only God could do. We can forgive a person for hurting us, but we don't have the authority to pardon someone for all the sins they've ever committed against God. That authority lies in God alone. Yet it is this kind of overarching forgiveness of all sins that Jesus bestows on people throughout his public ministry. It's no surprise that many of Jesus's Jewish contemporaries are outraged over this. When he says, for example, to a paralyzed man, "Your sins are forgiven you" (Lk 5:20), the scribes and Pharisees are shocked and call Jesus a blasphemer. They ask, "Who can forgive sins but God only?" (Lk 5:21).

Similarly, when one of the religious leaders in Jerusalem criticizes Jesus, saying, "Who do you think you are? Do you think you are better than Abraham?" he responds with this most remarkable statement about his identity, saying, "Truly, truly, I say to you, before Abraham was, I am" (Jn 8:58). "I Aм" (in Hebrew, "Yahweh") is God's Holy Name, which he has revealed to Moses (see Ex 3:14). So holy is God's name in the Bible that no Jew would ever utter it. A first-century Jew, hearing Jesus say "before Abraham was, I am," would understand Jesus to be alluding to the unutterable name of God and applying it to himself! Many of Jesus's hearers are appalled. In fact, they want to stone him to death for blasphemy (see Jn 8:58–59).

Jesus is markedly different from all other Jewish rabbis or other religious leaders the world has ever known. He doesn't just claim to be a teacher, a prophet, or a messenger from God. He makes himself the central issue of faith. He doesn't just offer a way to God or truth about God, but says, "*I am* the way, and the truth, and the life" (Jn 14:6, emphasis added). Similarly, he doesn't just call people to believe in God as other prophets and religious teachers throughout the centuries have done. He actually tells people to believe *in him*: "Whoever lives and believes in me shall never die" (Jn 11:26).

And this has dramatic consequences for our lives.

Just a Good Man?

Many people today—even some Christians—say that Jesus was just a good man, just one of many religious leaders the world has offered. But they are uncomfortable talking about Jesus as God. And we can understand why: If Jesus is God, then I must follow him. And that might mean making some changes to my life. But if I convince myself Jesus is just one of many spiritual teachers from whom we can learn, then I can pick and choose what teachings of Jesus fit my lifestyle and set aside those that challenge me to grow and to change. I don't have to outright reject that kind of warm-and-fuzzy Jesus. But I also don't have to follow him as a *disciple*.

But the real Jesus won't let us get away with that. He challenges us to make a choice. He repeatedly acts and speaks as God. So either he is who he claims to be or he's a very bad man, a liar who has deceived millions of people throughout the world into thinking he is God. Or, at best, he is a very confused man—someone who sincerely thinks he is God but is not. We can accept Jesus as Lord, we can accuse him of being a liar, or we can feel sorry for him as a deluded extremist or crazy man. But, as C. S. Lewis points out, it does not make any sense to say Jesus is merely a good man, a wise moral teacher, or a spiritual guide. Jesus doesn't give us that option.[1]

That now leads us back to the fundamental question Jesus posed some 2,000 years ago: "Who do you say that I am?" (Mt 16:15). Will you accept him as who he has claimed to be and welcome him as Lord of your life? That's a very personal question, but if you do welcome Jesus as the God who became man, then you are set to embark on the adventure of following him as a disciple.

Third, the Disciples Are Not Models of Perfection. They Are Models of a Process.

Do you ever feel that you're not progressing in the spiritual life? You repeatedly struggle with the same shortcomings. You keep bringing the same sins to Confession. You don't notice yourself growing in holiness. You might wonder, "How could I be a disciple? I'm not good enough."

If there's one thing the Gospels make clear, however, it is that the disciples are not models of perfection. They certainly are not chosen because they are smarter, more gifted, or more talented than others. Rather, the Gospels report their consistent fears, misunderstandings, failures, and weaknesses.

Just take the great St. Peter, for example. One moment he boldly declares to Jesus with great faith, "You are the Christ, the son of the living God" (Mt 16:16). The next moment he opposes Jesus's prophecy that he will go to Jerusalem to die, saying, "God forbid, Lord! This shall never happen to you" (Mt

---

[1] C. S. Lewis, *Mere Christianity* (New York: Macmillan, 1960), 55–56.

16:22). At the Last Supper, Peter declares that he would never leave Jesus and would be willing to die with him. Later that same night, Peter denies Jesus three times out of fear of being associated with him. Peter is definitely a work in progress, not a completed masterpiece from the get-go.

And that should be comforting for us. We can sometimes put the saints on a high pedestal and admire them from afar so much that we forget their humanness—that they were one of us and experienced many of the same challenges that we face in our walk with God. Instead, we tend to view the saints as superheroes with special magical powers we will never possess: some saints can stay up all night in prayer; others can levitate or bilocate; and others can wear hair shirts, throw themselves in rose bushes, and fast for forty days for penance. Meanwhile, we struggle just to wake up on time, say our prayers each day, and keep our rooms

> "The saints have not 'fallen from Heaven.' They are people like us, who also have complicated problems."
> —Pope Benedict XVI

clean. From this outlook, the saints might be impressive, but they seem to have nothing to do with our lives and the real struggles we face each day.

But it's important to keep in mind the *humanity* of the saints. To hear about the weaknesses of Peter, James, and John and other holy heroes throughout the ages can be helpful—not to celebrate their mistakes or lower the bar for our own spiritual lives, but to give us hope that the Jesus who worked with Peter's weakness and transformed him into a great saint can do the same with us.

That's one good reason we should study the lives of the disciples in Scripture and the lives of the saints in Church history. They are not models of a perfection that came all at once, but models of a lifelong process of gradual, ongoing conversion. They loved God, made heroic sacrifices, and gave themselves to the Lord in radical service. But they also had moments when they doubted. They lacked trust. They stumbled. They begged for mercy whenever they fell. And then they got back up again hoping in God's grace to help them. All along the way, the Lord was always walking beside them, inviting them to take the next step of faith, catching them when they fell, helping them get up, and encouraging them to walk again. Through this process, they were subtly being transformed—gradually, step-by-step, they were molded by Christ, changed by the Holy Spirit "into his likeness from one degree of glory to another" (2 Cor 3:18).

Pope Benedict XVI once described how this fact is very encouraging for us. "Hence there are also disputes, disagreements and controversies among saints. And I find this very comforting, because we see that the saints have not 'fallen from Heaven.' They are people like us, who also have complicated problems."[2]

Then he goes on to give a surprising but absolutely magnificent description of what it really means to become holy: "Holiness does not consist in never having erred or sinned. Holiness increases the capacity for conversion, for repentance, for willingness to start again and, especially, for reconciliation and forgiveness.... It is not the fact that we have never erred but our capacity for reconciliation and forgiveness which makes us saints. And we can all learn this way of holiness."[3]

---

[2] Pope Benedict XVI, General Audience (January 31, 2007).
[3] Ibid.

The disciples in the New Testament are not models of perfection. But they do model the process of becoming saints. The path to sanctity is not paved with perfection—with not making mistakes or never sinning—but with experiencing our many fears, faults, and failures; encountering God's mercy and grace ever anew; and humbly getting up and trying again. That, indeed, is a way of holiness we can all learn.

Fourth, Our Rabbi Dwells Within Us

Here we come to the most profound difference between disciples of Jesus and disciples of other rabbis.

As Christians, we have the ability to imitate our Master in a way no disciples of other rabbis were ever able to do. While other disciples may have carefully observed their rabbi's way of life and earnestly striven to emulate it, we have a unique advantage in that our Rabbi is not merely an example to study from the outside. *Our Rabbi abides within us*! Other disciples sought to walk in their master's footsteps, literally following him so closely that they would be covered with the dust of their rabbi. But we don't merely walk in our Rabbi's footsteps from behind. In a sense, he walks in our shoes, for Jesus, our Master, says that he will come to abide in us: "Abide in me, and I in you" (Jn 15:4).

> "Holiness does not consist in never having erred or sinned."
> —Pope Benedict XVI

This gift of Christ dwelling within us is what the Church calls "sanctifying grace"—a grace that sanctifies (*sanctify* means "to make holy.") We're going to take a closer look at this reality because it is a crucial key to discipleship. Understanding the power of grace—what it is, how it changes us, how we grow in it—can make all the difference for our growth as Christian disciples.

Amazing Grace

Christians often talk about grace. We say grace before meals. We hear the word "grace" at Mass. We pray for grace. We even sing hymns about how amazing it is. But what exactly is grace? And what difference does it make for our lives?

In short, sanctifying grace is Christ's divine life in us. The Son of God who became man comes to dwell within us, causing us to share in the divine life.[4] What's crucial here, however, is not to glance over those words as pious talk or abstract theological jargon but to appreciate the profound realism of all this. Let's take that in again: *the God of the universe comes to dwell within us*! Inside our souls, the life of the Son of God, through grace, is moving us, prompting us, and guiding us. It strengthens us to do what we could not do on our own. It heals us of our weaknesses, wounds, and sins. Through a slow, gradual, and subtle process, we are being changed to become ever more like our Rabbi, Jesus Christ.

A common analogy used in the Catholic tradition to explain the power of grace in our soul is that of the iron rod in the fire. When an iron rod is placed in fire, it starts to glow, turning red. It emits smoke. It becomes very hot. It begins to take on the qualities of fire. And that's what happens in our souls through sanctifying grace. It's as if our souls are transformed by the fire of the Holy Spirit. We slowly begin to be more patient and forgiving like Jesus, courageous and generous like Jesus, humble and loving like Jesus. Over time, we begin to take on the qualities of Christ.

---

[4] *Catechism of the Catholic Church*, nos. 1997–98 (hereafter cited as *CCC*).

Growing in Grace

Is there an area of your life where you're struggling? A certain relationship that's not going well? A certain weakness that keeps you from being the person you're called to be? A habitual sin that you just can't seem to get rid of? If you're striving to be more virtuous, more generous to God, then you need to pray for grace.

Grace enables us to live and to love *supernaturally*—beyond what our human nature can do on its own. So if you want to live life at a higher level, if you want to love your God, your friends, your spouse, and your children to the fullest, then you want to grow in grace. With Christ's life in you, you can begin to love God and the people in your life in a way that you could not do on your own, for it is Christ loving them through you.

This is why we need to seek God's grace in our lives: so that we can become ever more like Christ. As we'll see in Part Two, we grow in grace through frequenting the Sacraments, through a regular prayer life, through asking for grace, and through cooperating with grace by doing good deeds. The more we respond to God's graces, the more graces he will give us. And if we continue to grow in God's grace, we will be changed, so much so that we can say with St. Paul, "It is no longer I who live, but Christ who lives in me" (Gal 2:20).

Indeed, we don't just walk in the dust of our Rabbi, following him from behind. Our good Rabbi Jesus abides in us and wants to reproduce his life in us, changing us from the inside out.

Fifth, Jesus Calls Us to Take Up our Cross Daily

"If any man would come after me, let him deny himself and take up his cross daily and follow me" (Lk 9:23).

The idea of taking up your cross would have been utterly shocking in first-century Judaism. Far from being a pious religious symbol as it is today, the cross in Jesus's time would have been a painful reminder of the most humiliating, shameful, torturous way of dying: Roman crucifixion. "Take up your cross" is like saying to modern people, "Take up your guillotine and follow me" or "Take up your electric chair and follow me." Why would anyone want to join a movement that has a symbol of death at its center?

Yet Jesus explains that it is only by dying that we will find true life. When we die to our self-centered interests, die to our pride, die to our desire for control, die to our lust, die to our own will, we actually discover a richer existence, a life lived for others and for God, a life of love. When we grasp after our own glory, pleasure, and comfort, we become entrapped in self-interest and never experience the joys of authentic love, *agape*. "For whoever would save his life will lose it; and whoever loses his life for my sake, he will save it" (Lk 9:24).

Vatican II summed up this mysterious law of self-giving: man finds himself only by making himself a sincere gift to others. Jesus modeled this on the Cross—he gave his life completely as a gift to the Father for the sake of our salvation. We're called to conform our lives to this total self-giving *agape* love, taking up our own crosses daily and following Jesus.

How do we do this? We can each die to self in countless small ways: we can wake up early to have time for prayer, even though we'd rather hit the snooze button; we can forgive someone who hurt us; we can hold back our temper with a child who made a mess for the tenth time in the last hour; we can joyfully bear with an annoying habit of our spouse; we can let others be at the center of attention; we can refuse to let ourselves become frustrated or discouraged when things don't go our way; we can stand up for an unpopular moral truth; we can praise others and humbly seek to be unnoticed. In these and other small ways of dying to self, we become ever more conformed to Jesus Christ Crucified. And in doing so, we discover a deeper meaning and purpose to our lives: the way of love. Indeed, the crosses we face aren't merely problems to be solved or sacrifices to be offered up. They are opportunities to encounter Christ Crucified anew and grow in his love.

Each day, in fact, Jesus gives us many opportunities to show our love for him and bear the Cross. Some crosses are bigger than others. Some are more difficult to bear than others. But we never have to carry these crosses on our own. Jesus is there with us, helping us carry the Cross and drawing us ever more into his own sacrificial, self-giving love. If a fully-trained disciple becomes like his teacher, we Christian disciples must become ever more like Christ Crucified, which means being transformed by his total, self-giving love on the Cross.

Reflection Questions

- How has God used certain people or circumstances in your life to draw you closer to him? How does knowing that God seeks us out and takes the initiative in our discipleship impact the way you view your friendship with him?

- In this chapter, we saw how Pope Emeritus Benedict XVI said that "holiness does not consist in not making mistakes or never sinning." How might this challenge your view of holiness? How might knowing that the saints were works in progress—men and women who struggled with sin but had the capacity for conversion and the will to try again and again—offer you encouragement in your own walk with the Lord?

PART TWO

The Encounter

We must do everything in our power, give without counting the cost, practice virtue at every opportunity, deny ourselves constantly, prove our love by all kinds of attentions and marks of affection, in a word, do all the good deeds in our power for the love of God. But since all that is really very little, it is important to place all our trust in him who alone sanctifies all deeds, and can sanctify without them....That is what "the little way of childhood" is all about.

—St. Thérèse of Lisieux

Meeting God in the Valley

Many parents remember their babies' first step. I'm just as fascinated by a child's first jump.

Our sixteen-month-old has recently been attempting to jump for the first time. The older siblings make a circle around her, cheering her on and modeling for her how to do it. They all bend their knees, get low to the ground, and then suddenly spring upward while exhorting their little sister, "Jump! You can do it! Jump!"

The child just loves all the attention and excitement! She smiles, laughs, and then tries to imitate them. She bends her knees, too. She gets low to the ground. She locks into position and attempts the great launch upward. And then?

Nothing. Her two feet never leave the ground.

She smiles and tries a second time. Still no takeoff. After three or four more attempts, she's not laughing anymore. Her smile has turned to a look of frustration. The more her siblings encourage her, the sadder she becomes with each failed attempt. She simply can't do this jumping thing.

We disciples can sometimes feel the same. We want to be better at prayer. We want to root out our bad habits and sins. We sincerely strive to imitate Christ. But we can't. No matter how hard we try, we find ourselves struggling with the same weaknesses. We want to rise up to God, but feel stuck and frustrated and wonder if our spiritual life will ever take off.

Indeed, the process of being conformed to Christ is not an easy one. And it doesn't happen overnight. Through the course of life, we slowly learn what it means to live like

"Apart from me you can do *nothing.*" (Jn 15:5)

Jesus, how to follow him, and how to be more virtuous and grow in holiness. And all along the way, we learn a most important lesson: the whole process of being changed into Christ's likeness is ultimately God's work.

We may know this in our heads, "Yes, I am a sinner, filled with many weaknesses. I need God's help. I can't do this on my own." *But do we know this deep in our hearts?* Do we live from this conviction day by day, moment by moment, in all we do? Being formed as Christian disciples involves learning how to live from this fundamental truth about how we are completely dependent on God and learning how to rely on God's grace for all we do, not just "in times of need." After all, Jesus didn't say, "Apart from me you can do only fifty percent." He said, "Apart from me you can do *nothing*" (Jn 15:5, emphasis added). Only someone who is utterly convinced of this truth and who lives from this truth—not just in his head but at the core of his being—can fully progress as a disciple of the Lord.

A Masterpiece in Three Movements

God's work of conforming us to the image of his Son usually takes a lifetime. But we can discern three ongoing movements in this beautiful process of discipleship. These are not stages or levels in the spiritual life, but movements that many saints in various ways describe as happening time after time throughout their lives as they sought deeper union with God. Think of these as three movements in the spiritual life that are part of our ongoing conversion, our ever-deeper transformation in imitating Christ.

1. The Upward Struggle
2. Falling Back
3. Lifted by God's Grace[1]

This chapter will focus on the first two movements: *our struggle up to God* (our earnest striving to live like Christ) and our *falling back* in failure and weakness. No matter how hard we try, we come face-to-face with our inability to live the Christian life as well as we'd like to. We will see that it is here that God wants to meet us—in our weakness, as we really are, not as we'd like to be.

And if we allow God to meet us here in our poverty, at this low point with all our faults and weaknesses, we can discover a third crucial movement in the spiritual life— one that is a surer and more direct way up to God: being *lifted by God's grace*. Indeed, if we allow ourselves to meet God in such humility, we can encounter him in a powerful way that changes us and lifts us up to him. This third movement will be explored over the next three chapters, which focus on an encounter with God's love (chapter 7), with his forgiveness (chapter 8), and with his healing grace (chapter 9).

---

[1] I am thankful to Fr. Paul Murray, OP, for opening up these themes in his classes, conversations with him, and his writings. For more, see, for example, his *In the Grip of Light: The Dark and Bright Journey of Christian Contemplation* (London: Bloomsbury, 2012).

The Upward Struggle

First, the *upward struggle*. Before living as disciples of Jesus, most of us didn't truly recognize the extent of our sins and weaknesses and how they were affecting our lives. We weren't intentionally striving to improve our spiritual lives and imitate Christ. We just muddled through life, either sincerely having no idea how far off we were or desperately trying to convince ourselves that we were living a good enough life and that we were happy.

But something changes when Jesus becomes more of a priority. Our faith takes off, and we start trying to live a better life. We want to follow Jesus and take his message seriously. We learn new things about the faith and begin to notice areas in our lives that need to be different.

We want to change. We want to be better. We set out to do whatever we can to root out these sins and grow in virtue. We make new resolutions. "I'll never do that again." We pray for God's help. We sincerely want to do whatever it takes to shake off these bad habits and live like Christ.

This is the upward movement that is sparked inside the disciple. We're seeking God, intentionally striving to live more like Jesus. Indeed, this is the crucial first step in Christian discipleship: the disciple purposely seeking to imitate the Master.

Falling Back

But this first step up isn't enough. No matter how much we set our minds to it and try with all our might to change, we will still run up against our own limitations and weaknesses. Even if we adopt a Nike spirituality ("Just do it!"), we won't be able to conquer all the vices that weigh us down. And even if we develop a three-year strategic plan to grow in holiness, we're probably not going to gain two-and-a-half virtues each month. This is the second step: *falling back.*

Once we sincerely start trying to walk in Jesus's footsteps as disciples, we quickly realize how far we are falling behind. We make some improvements but then fall back into our old patterns. We try hard to stop committing certain sins but find ourselves unable to change.

Why is this happening? We're supposed to be serious Christians: committed disciples, "on-fire" Catholics, dynamic followers of the Lord. We even pray, frequent the Sacraments, and take time to learn more about the Faith. Why are we not as holy as we should be? We still get impatient with our spouses and kids. We still struggle with purity. We're not as generous with our time and our possessions as we know we should be. We still get discouraged when things aren't going well, complain when we're uncomfortable, and gossip about other people when they frustrate us. I sincerely want to be more Christ-like. Why can't I change?

Three Options

It's with this difficult realization that the soul has the opportunity to grow like never before. But we must be careful to choose the right path forward. Three options lie ahead of us.

One path to avoid is the way of *despair*: We are so overwhelmed by our weaknesses that we think we can never change. We've tried and tried, but nothing works. We think that our sins are too great and that we're somehow unforgivable. Or we're just not confident that God can help us do what we can't do on our own. So we give up. We stop trying. We give in to our weaknesses and stop following Jesus as disciples. St. Bernard of Clairvaux explains that this is what happens when people don't know how much God loves them and wants to help them. "If he does not know how good God is, how kind and gentle, how willing to pardon, will not his sensually-inspired reason argue with him and say: 'What are you doing? . . . Your sins are too grave and too many. . . . A lifetime's habits are not easily conquered.' Dismayed by these and similar arguments, the unhappy man quits the struggle, not knowing how easily God's omnipotent goodness could overthrow all these obstacles."[2]

A second path to avoid is the way of *impatience*. We can be impatient with our weaknesses and beat ourselves up for our many shortcomings. Sometimes we wish we didn't have to depend on God's mercy so much. We wish we were better. We wish we could present ourselves to God "pure and spotless," already holy, not needing his forgiveness, mercy, and healing. "I know I need God's help a little, but I wish I didn't need it this much!" We're discouraged and upset when we're not as virtuous as we'd like to be, when we're not making the spiritual progress we'd like to be making, and when we're still plagued by the same old sins that won't go away.

On the surface, this frustration with self might appear to be noble: a sign of a soul longing for deeper union with God, a sign of humility as the soul recognizes his faults: "I can't believe I did that again! Why am I not getting any better? I keep falling into the same sins." But we also must see that this agitation might be less about sorrow over one's sins and more about pride. In some cases, as spiritual writer Father Jacques Philippe

---

[2]   St. Bernard of Clairvaux, *On the Song of Songs* II, trans. Kilian Walsh (Kalamazoo, MI: Cistercian Publications, 1976), 38:1.

explains, "We are not sad and discouraged so much because God was offended, but because the ideal image that we have of ourselves has been brutally shaken. Our pain is very often that of wounded pride!"[3] In fact, notice how much attention is on self. "*I* can't believe *I* did that." The spiritually proud soul is not looking up to God and throwing himself into the Father's merciful arms. Rather, he's dismayed that he's not performing at the spiritual level to which he aspires. His image of himself as a more advanced Christian has been shattered.

Let's not follow this path of impatience, which gets us to focus too much on self and might have spiritual pride at its roots. Instead, when we face our many sins and failures, let's humbly accept our poverty and turn all our attention to God in loving surrender: "Jesus, I'm sorry. I've sinned again. But this is the truth of who I am: a weak sinner who can do nothing on his own. I ask your forgiveness. I'll sincerely try to do better next time. And I trust in your grace to heal me in the future. In the meantime, I pray that my stumbles along the way will make me even more aware of my need for you, more grateful for your mercy, and more patient and compassionate with others when I'm affected by their faults."

But God wants to meet us right now *as we really are*, not as we'd *like* to be.

Lifted by God's Grace

This leads us to the third path, the path of true *humility*, which is the way of the disciple. Something St. Thérèse once wrote to her sister Céline illuminates this path.

---

[3] Jacques Philippe, *Searching for and Maintaining Peace* (New York: Alba House, 2004), 58.

Like many Christians, Céline came to that moment of feeling discouraged by her many faults and weaknesses that kept her from a closer relationship with God. She was overwhelmed by the long way she knew she had yet to go in her pursuit of holiness. It was like climbing a steep mountain that reached into the clouds. But Thérèse encouraged her and helped her to see she didn't have to climb the tall mountain up to God. God would come down to meet her—if she let him: "You wish to scale a mountain and the good God wants to make you descend; he is waiting for you low down in the fertile valley of humility."[4]

What a beautiful image! Too often, we want to climb the mountain of sanctity and present ourselves to God in some ideal way—perfect, holy, virtuous, devout. But God wants to meet us right now *as we really are*, not as we'd *like* to be. He wants to meet the real me, as I really am, filled with some noble qualities but also tainted by many imperfections, wounds, and sins—not some other idyllic version of myself that doesn't exist yet. That's why the first step up the mountain of sanctity is actually a step down—down to "the fertile valley of humility."

When we dare to go to the valley of humility and allow ourselves to meet God as we are, we can ascend the mountain in a most secure and direct way. For God is not waiting up at the summit for you to find your way up to him. He's waiting down in the valley to meet you as you are, so that he can lift you up to the heights of the spiritual life, far beyond what you could ever do on your own. This

---

[4] St. Thérèse of Lisieux, *The Little Way: Counsels and Reminiscences of the Little Flower* (Charlotte, NC: St. Michael's Press, 1997), 11.

is the third movement in the spiritual life: *being lifted by God's grace.*

Indeed, as we will see next, three amazing things can happen when we encounter God in the valley this way. First, we come to know at a much deeper level how loved we are by God—not for what we do, but for who we are even with all our frailty and weakness. Second, we experience God's forgiveness. And third, we learn ever more to rely on his grace, his healing power. Indeed, the fastest and surest way up the mountain of sanctity is not arduous ascending by one's own effort but allowing God to lift you up.

Reflection Questions

- What sometimes keeps you from facing the honest truth about yourself and allowing God to meet you as you are, with all your sins, wounds, and poverty? Is it pride? Not wanting to admit your faults? Not wanting to change? Fear that you won't like what you see? Fear that God will reject you?

- Do you ever get discouraged or frustrated with your weaknesses and failures? How might this be a form of pride? What is a better way to respond to our faults and sins?

Drunk with Love

In my young adult years, I often heard priests, teachers, and campus ministers say, "God loves you." But, to be honest, this fundamental message didn't captivate my attention or sink into my soul. "Yeah, yeah... I know God loves me. Of course. He loves everyone. Okay, can we get on to the deeper topics now, like the Eucharist or prayer?"

God's love for us is something we might know in our heads. But it's not something most of us fully grasp in our hearts. Yet, if we aspire to move forward in discipleship, we absolutely must encounter this divine love anew—not in an abstract way ("True or False: God loves you") or in a children's song way ("Jesus loves me, this I know..."), but personally, profoundly, in a way that turns our world upside down.

Especially in a utilitarian age, we have been trained from our youth to think that love is something based on what we do for others. How useful we are to others, how we make them feel, or how much fun or enjoyment we give them— these are what give our lives value and get other people to love us. Our identity and sense of self are wholly dependent on how well we perform and how we are viewed by others.

71

Children sometimes grow up feeling loved by their parents for what they achieve in school, on the field, and in their dozens of extracurricular activities. Young people growing up in a digital age are trained to see their value as being based on how well they artificially project themselves, on how many "likes" and comments they get, and on how many "friends" or followers they acquire on social media. Authentic friendship based on two people who seek what's best for each other is hard to find. Everyone's in it for themselves. Even in many romantic relationships today, couples are not truly committed to each other—they're just committed to the good feelings, emotions, and pleasures they get from each other. Once those feelings and emotions fade, or they can get more pleasure from someone else, the relationship ends and they move on to the next person.

So, when many people feel tremendous pressure to constantly perform well, never to misstep, and desperately to keep up a certain image, it's no wonder their relationships and identity are built on such shaky ground. Even for some of the most outwardly confident, competent, successful people, the idea of being some-one who is truly lovable—of being loved as a person for one's own sake—is hard to even imagine. "You mean, me? With all my problems? I could experience authentic, lasting, committed love just for who I am, as I am? I didn't know such love existed!"

And yet it's only by coming to know how much my God loves me, as I am, with all my faults and shortcomings, that I can come to see reality properly—most particularly, the reality of my life properly. As Pope St. John Paul II says, "*We are not the sum of our weaknesses and failures*; we are the sum of our Father's love for us and our real capacity to become the image of his Son."[1]

---

[1]   Pope St. John Paul II, homily, 17th World Youth Day Solemn Mass (July 28, 2002).

Prodigals

God often uses moments when we are broken down and stripped of all that we think supports us to bring us to a deeper experience of his love. Even many of us Christians go through life relying on our talent, hard work, popularity, success, looks, or ability to keep others pleased to give us the sense that our lives have meaning. We might know in our heads that there's more to life than all this, but we still turn to these supports as the foundation for our happiness. But when all is taken away—when we experience broken relationships, health problems, job problems, marriage problems, being overwhelmed by the demands of raising children, or other sufferings—and none of our normal supports are working, the only thing left to cling to is God. It's then that we come to know God's love as more than an abstract theory. We *experience* his love personally supporting us, holding us together, and helping us through.

> It's only by coming to know how much my God loves me, as I am, with all my faults and shortcomings, that I can come to see reality properly.

I've had many priests, religious sisters, and lay pastoral workers tell me how they've seen this moment over and over again as the crucial turning point for people's relationships with God. One priest who works with young adults described how many of them feel like trash inside, especially when they admit not having it all together and having struggled with some serious sin. But after a period of time in helping them through their challenges and accompanying them through the process of healing and forgiveness, this priest asks them, "What do you think of the way I responded when you opened up about your struggle?" They all reply with something like, "I couldn't believe it. You didn't judge me. You didn't look down on me or think less of me. You didn't reject me. You stayed with me all the way." Then the priest says to them, "If that's how I—with all my weaknesses and all my human shortcomings—responded, think about how the God whose love is perfect looks at you. He loves you completely. He stays with you."

At that moment of suddenly realizing the depths of God's love for them, many young adults melt. It turns their world upside down. They've never seen themselves as loved in this way. In fact, it's a crucial aspect of their conversion: not just their turning away from sinful actions, but their turning away from false views of God and of themselves.

The Father's Embrace

This is also the climactic turning point in the story of the Prodigal Son. A son who rejects his father, takes his family's inheritance early, leaves home for a distant land, and squanders the inheritance on immoral living comes to experience his father's love in a totally new way. Many people think the son's point of conversion comes when he is living as a slave, hungry and poor, and decides to return to his father. He says to himself, "How many of my father's hired servants have bread enough and to spare, but I perish here with hunger! I will arise and go to my father, and I will say to him, 'Father, I have sinned against heaven and before you; I am no longer worthy to be called your son; treat me as one of your hired servants'" (Lk 15:17–19).

But another level of conversion happens when he arrives home and encounters something completely unexpected. The son admits his sin, is truly sorry, and turns back to the father—a good first step—but it isn't enough. He isn't turning back as a beloved son. He doesn't view himself as being worthy of that anymore. After all he has done to shame the family, how can he be called a son? The possibility of receiving his father's love isn't even on his radar screen. He deserves to be treated as a slave, and the best he can hope for is that the father will pardon him and accept him as a hired worker. As long as he does what he's told and does good work, he can earn the boss's approval and merit his wages. That's why, as soon as he meets his father, he starts saying those words, "I am no longer worthy to be called your son ... "

But the father will have absolutely none of this. He cuts his son off and will not allow him to continue his self-effacing sentence. The father embraces him—nothing that the son has done can make the father turn away from him. The father declares the truth that the son can't see in himself. "This *my son* was dead, and is alive again; he was lost, and is found" (Lk 15:24, emphasis added). The parable of the prodigal son is about more than turning away from sin and finding forgiveness. It's also about turning away from the incorrect picture we have of God and of ourselves. At heart, the conversion in this story involves our very identity as beloved children of God ("This my son...") and a most unexpected love that turns our world upside down. As Pope St. John Paul II explains, conversion is always the fruit of rediscovering the Father.[2]

Drunk with Love

If we dare to meet God in the valley, we come to experience at a much deeper level how much the Father loves us—as

---

[2] Pope St. John Paul II, encyclical letter *Dives in misericordia* (November 30, 1980), no. 13.

we are, with all our thousands of fears, worries, hurts, suspicions, sins, weaknesses, and failures. God's love for us is unconditional. It's not dependent on how we perform. It's not based on how many prayers we recite, how well we keep our Lenten resolutions, how well our kids behave at Mass, and how often we avoid falling into sexual sin. God loves us, as we are, with all our messiness. He longs for us. He thirsts for us. As we are. Not as we'd like to be.

Yes, Jesus calls us to repent when we sin. And he calls us to the highest standard of holiness: "You, therefore, must be perfect, as your heavenly Father is perfect" (Mt 5:48). To do that, he needs to forgive us, heal us, change us, and sanctify us. There's certainly a lot of work to be done in our souls! *But none of that can happen in a deep, lasting way until we embrace two fundamental truths*: the truth about ourselves and the truth about how God sees us. We must face the truth about all our tragic weaknesses and wounds. And then we must see ourselves, even with those failures, in the way God sees us: with a surprising gentleness, patience, and mercy and with a total, unconditional love that we don't think we deserve.

> It's not about winning God's approval or earning his love by doing enough good Catholic things.

And that's the whole point. It's not about winning God's approval or earning his love by doing enough good Catholic things. When we meet God in the valley of humility, we encounter a most unexpected love, a totally free gift that is completely different from our ordinary human experience.

It's this encounter with God's personal love that amazed St. Catherine of Siena, who once called God "drunk with love." It overwhelmed St. Teresa of Calcutta, who couldn't comprehend how the infinite God loved someone so weak and small as she: "That God is high, transcendent, all-powerful, almighty, I can understand that because I am so small. But that God has become small, and that he thirsts for my love, *begs* for it—I *cannot* understand it, I *cannot* understand it, I *cannot* understand it."[3] It made St. Augustine regret that he learned to love God so late. It made St. Dominic weep all night in the chapel. And it drove many saints to the ends of the earth to share this love with souls who didn't know God.

We're not talking here about merely recognizing the truth that "God loves me" in the abstract, on a catechism quiz. And we're not talking about merely being loved as part of group ("God loves everyone. I'm part of 'everyone'; therefore, God has to love me, too.") No, we're talking about God loving you in a unique and unrepeatable way, for he longs for you personally, individually. We're talking about having your world turned upside down and your view of yourself completely changed, for you begin to see yourself, perhaps for the first time in your life, not in terms of what you do for others nor in terms of your many faults and wounds, but in the way God sees you. And this is a crucial step in maturing as a Christian disciple. It may require many years, in some cases a lifetime, to be reprogrammed from the damage caused by our utilitarian mindset. You can't earn love, whether from a parent, a friend, a spouse, or a boss. And you certainly can't earn it from God. It has to be received.

[3] Paul Murray, *I Loved Jesus in the Night: Teresa of Calcutta* (Brewster, Massachusetts: Paraclete Press, 2008), 73. Emphasis in original.

But once this divine love is received, welcomed, and embraced, it changes everything. Indeed, this encounter with God's love for you, for who you are as you are, is a step in helping you see reality correctly. It is from this fundamental conviction that a soul finds true identity: You are a beloved son or daughter of God, and nothing you've done or may do can change that. Your heavenly Father delights in and embraces you.

Living from this embrace gives a much more solid foundation for one's life. Many of us, unfortunately, go through life with a fragile, artificial confidence—fragile and artificial because it's based on ourselves (our abilities, our looks, our reputations, how we perform, how we keep people around us happy). None of these things can provide a secure, lasting peace and happiness for our lives. But when we deeply encounter God's love, we begin to build our lives on solid ground. Our confidence is based not on ourselves but on God's love for us. When this happens, love is what moves us in all we do, not our trying to perform well to earn love from others or from God.

In closing, consider the following striking words from St. Teresa of Calcutta to the sisters in her religious community, the Missionaries of Charity. Late in her life, one urgent concern she had for her sisters was that many had not allowed themselves to truly encounter Jesus's love for them. Her pleading words certainly apply to us as well. If she had those concerns for these amazing sisters who give up everything for Jesus and serve the poorest of the poor around the world, imagine what she might say to you and me!

> "I worry some of you still have not really met Jesus—one-to-one—you and Jesus alone."
> —St. Teresa of Calcutta

I worry some of you still have not really met Jesus—one-to-one—you and Jesus alone. We may spend time in chapel—but have you seen with the eyes of your soul how He looks at you with love? Do you really know the living Jesus—not from books, but from being with Him in your heart? Have you heard the living words He speaks to you?

Ask for the grace, He is longing to give it. Never give up this daily intimate contact with Jesus as a real living person—not just an idea.

Be careful of all that can block that personal being in touch with the living Jesus. The hurts of life, and sometimes your own mistakes—[may] make you feel it is impossible that Jesus really loves you, is really clinging to you. This is a danger for all of you. And so sad, because it is completely opposite of what Jesus is really wanting, waiting to tell you.

Not only He loves you, even more—He longs for you. He misses you when you don't come close. He thirsts for you. He loves you always, even when you don't feel worthy. Even if you are not accepted by others, even by yourself sometimes—He is the one who always accepts you.

My children, you don't have to be different for Jesus to love you. Only believe—You are precious to Him. Bring all you are suffering to His feet—only open your heart to be loved by Him as you are. He will do the rest.[4]

---

[4] From St. Teresa of Calcutta's "Varanasi Letter" in Joseph Langford, *Mother Teresa's Secret Fire* (Huntington, IN: Our Sunday Visitor, 2008), 54–55.

Reflection Questions

- Put yourself in the story of the prodigal son: Do you tend to see yourself as the son saw himself ("I'm not worthy to be called your son")? Or more as the father sees him—as a beloved son?

- What line from St. Teresa of Calcutta's prayer struck you and applies to your life most? What do you think God is trying to tell you through that line?

Forgiven

Think about your most hidden sin. Your most embarrassing weakness. It could be something you did a long time ago or something you're struggling with right now. Imagine that suddenly this secret, humiliating fault of yours comes out into the public, and everyone knows about it: your family, friends, coworkers, neighbors, parishioners. How do you feel?

Ashamed. Angry. Afraid. Ashamed over what you did. Ashamed you gave into temptation. Angry at yourself for your weakness. Angry that it became public. Afraid of what others think of you. Afraid over what will happen now that everyone knows.

Then imagine that, just at that moment, Jesus appears right in front of you. He looks you straight in the eye and confronts you with your sin. He says, "I know what you did."

But instead of coming to point his finger and condemn you, he goes on to give you a way out—a way to start all over again. Picture him saying to you, "I know what you did. I know what you're doing now. And I still love you. I don't condemn you. I forgive you. Go and sin no more."

That's basically what happens to the woman who is caught in adultery in chapter eight of John's Gospel. She has a serious

sin that is brought out into the light. Thrown before Jesus and
the leaders in Jerusalem, she is accused of adultery and her
community threatens to stone her to death. She probably has
many of the emotions we could relate to if our most hidden sins
were exposed. She probably feels alone, ashamed, afraid, and
filled with regret. She probably is already "throwing stones" at
herself, so to speak, even before the Jewish leaders threaten to
throw actual rocks at her for her punishment.

But just at that moment of self-condemnation and despair,
when she thinks all is lost, Jesus comes and does the most
unexpected thing. Jesus, the Lord and Judge of the universe,
comes not to issue a legal sentence. He comes not to condemn
her or punish her for having broken the Law. Instead, he
comes to forgive her and offers her a second chance, a whole
new start in life: "Neither do I condemn you; go, and do not
sin again" (Jn 8:11).

And Jesus wants to do the same with us. You see, the
woman's story is our story. We all have our own tragic stories
of sin and failure and the burden of guilt, shame, fear, and hurt
that come with that. Jesus wants to lift those burdens. He so
much wants to shower his mercy upon us, forgive our sins, and
give us a new start. He is the God of countless second chances.
He doesn't come as a prosecuting attorney, accusing us: "You
are terrible. You shouldn't even be called a Christian. You will
never change. Why do you even bother trying?" That's not the
voice of God. That's the voice of the devil, trying to discourage
us and get us to condemn ourselves—in fact, the devil's name,
"Satan," means "accuser." No, our God is on our side, rooting
for us, strengthening us, and inviting us to turn back to him
whenever we fall.

Jesus still calls us to follow the moral law. He told the
woman, "Go, and do not sin again." And we must repent any

time we fall and take our sins to Confession. But remember how much God thirsts for us. He wants to remove whatever obstacles hinder our relationship with him. That's why he is so willing to forgive. All we have to do is turn to him, tell him we're sorry, and sincerely try to be better.

This process of trying to live like Christ, falling short of the mark, and encountering Jesus's love and forgiveness is at the heart of our discipleship. It is through this up-and-down process that God does his work in us, reminding us of how small and weak we really are and of how great and strong his love is for us. We encounter a love that sets us free. We become free not just from our sins, but also from our fears, hurts, and self-condemnation.

She probably is already "throwing stones" at herself.

Along the way, we slowly learn to trust more in this love and less in our own ability. In this manner, God molds us and prepares us for the third and most amazing thing that happens when we meet God in the valley of humility: We experience a power that changes us and enables us to live like Christ—to live supernaturally, beyond what we could do on our own. This is the healing power of God's grace.

Reflection Questions

- Put yourself in the story of the woman caught in adultery. Imagine your sin being exposed but Jesus looking at you with love, saying, "Neither do I condemn you." How would that make you feel? How might that change the way you view yourself before God?

- Mercy and truth go together. That's why Jesus also tells the woman, "Go and sin no more." Imagine Jesus looking you square in the eye and saying those words to you. What sin of yours do you think Jesus would be referring to the most? How might his words strengthen your resolve to avoid this sin in the future?

Real Healing, Real Change

Jesus doesn't just want to forgive us. He wants to change us. He doesn't merely want to pardon us for our trespasses, like a judge would do. He wants to heal us of the roots of sin, like a doctor, so we can live life to the fullest and not be weighed down by our many weaknesses.

But the problem today is that many of us don't really believe we can be healed. Yes, we say we believe in a God who hears our prayers and can work wonders in our souls. But deep down we're not convinced. We think we have too many problems. Our lives are too complex for God to fix. Some of our hurts and bad habits run so deep that, as Pope Francis says, we consider "our illness, our sins, to be incurable, things that cannot be healed or forgiven.... We don't believe that there is a chance for redemption; for a hand to raise you up; for an embrace to save you, forgive you, pick you up, flood you with infinite, patient, indulgent love; to put you back on your feet."[1]

But the same Jesus who gave sight to the blind, cured the sick, and helped the lame to walk wants to work miracles in

---

[1] Pope Francis, *The Name of God Is Mercy* (New York: Image, 2016), 16.

us—if we let him. He wants to cure us of whatever blindness keeps us from seeing our lives accurately. He wants to heal us of whatever sins hinder us from following him. And in the areas of our lives where we feel helpless, paralyzed, or completely unable to change, he wants to liberate us and empower us to pick up our mats and walk again.

These are the kinds of little miracles Jesus works in ordinary souls all the time. But they are even more significant than calming storms or parting seas. For when God heals our pride, our fears, our addictions, our troubled marriages, our wounds from childhood, he manifests his power not only over nature, but over sin and the effects of sin. In the process, eternal souls that last longer than any storm or sea are changed, and the angels in Heaven rejoice, for God is molding us into his image.

But these little miracles usually don't happen in an instant. They're often the result of a slow process in which change occurs subtly, incrementally, over a long period of time without our even noticing. Progress seems negligible. You wonder if you'll ever shake this illness. Then one day you find yourself in the same situation in which you have failed the previous ninety-nine times, but this time, much to your surprise, you notice yourself acting differently. It's as if you're outside yourself watching yourself do something you've never done before. You know it's not you doing it. Jesus has worked a change in you.

St. Thérèse's Conversion Story

That's what happened when St. Thérèse had her conversion moment. Have you ever heard her conversion story? It's not a dramatic tale that would turn into a best-selling book or generate many television interviews. It's probably not even one that would be told over and over again on Catholic radio. But it's a conversion story we can all relate to: one about an ordinary person, struggling with an ordinary weakness, and God's changing her in a simple and subtle yet life-transforming way.

Thérèse is the youngest child in her family and loses her mother when she was four and a half years old. And this tragedy leaves its mark on her. Before her mother's death, Thérèse is a confident, outgoing, joyful little girl. But after her mother dies, she becomes excessively shy and emotionally sensitive. She tries to change but cannot overcome her hypersensitivities. Especially if she perceives she is causing anyone difficulty, she is greatly saddened. And this weakness itself depresses her. She often cries at the slightest bit of trouble and then cries for having cried.

After years of battling this weakness, however, Thérèse finally experiences a profound change in her soul that makes her confident and in control of her emotions from that moment on. She describes this as the moment of her "complete conversion."

It is Christmas Eve in 1886. She is fourteen years old. The family comes home from Midnight Mass, and Thérèse brings her shoes to the fireplace where her father has the Christmas Eve custom of putting little presents in them each year. As they are going up the stairs, she and her older sister Céline hear their father say something that would normally have sent Thérèse into an emotional downward spiral. Worn out after the long evening, their father notices the shoes at the fireplace and complains to himself about having to fill them at this late hour for his daughter who should have already outgrown this childhood tradition. He says to himself, "Well, fortunately, this will be the last year!"

These words pierce Thérèse's heart. Her eyes start to well up. Céline, knowing how much this pains her sister, says, "Oh, Thérèse, don't go downstairs; it would cause you too much grief to look at your slippers right now!" But at that moment, Thérèse notices a change inside her. She rises above her emotions and acts as if she has not heard what was said.

> Forcing back my tears, I descended the stairs rapidly; controlling the poundings of my heart, I took my slippers and placed them in front of Papa, and withdrew all the objects joyfully. I had the happy appearance of a Queen. Having regained his own cheerfulness, Papa was laughing; Céline believed it was all a dream! Fortunately, it was a sweet reality; Thérèse had discovered once again the strength of soul which she had lost at the age of four and a half, and she was to preserve it forever!

Thérèse explains that it was Jesus who changed her heart. "The work I had been unable to do in ten years was done by Jesus in one instant."[2]

Thérèse's experience that night is just one example of the kind of simple yet profound miracles Jesus works in ordinary souls. For her, it was overcoming her sensitive emotions. For others, it might be learning to control their tongues, guard their eyes, or manage their tempers. You find yourself in situations of temptation, but surprisingly something within you helps you withhold those critical words, turn away from those impure images, or hold back your anger. You know it wasn't your normal self. It was Jesus working through you.

For other souls, it might be not resenting a spouse or acting charitably to those who are hurtful. Instead of responding to a hurt by building up yet another wall in your marriage

---

[2]   St. Thérèse of Lisieux, *Story of a Soul*, trans. John Clarke (Washington: ICS Publications, 1972), 98.

("She'll never change" or "He just doesn't understand me"), something within you inspires you this time to give your spouse the benefit of the doubt ("She probably didn't mean that" or "I bet he didn't realize what he was doing.") When you're hurt by something a coworker or family member says, instead of being angry or dwelling on the hurt, you feel motivated to offer a sincere prayer for that person, recognizing that person probably has a lot of hurts of his or her own. You say a prayer like Jesus did on the Cross, "Father, forgive them; for they know not what they do" (Lk 23:34). Where did this newfound inner strength and mercy come from? You know it wasn't you. It was the Holy Spirit placing this idea in your heart.

Why Ten Years?

Some of us might wonder why it takes so much time to be healed. Why it might take ten years to experience change like it did for Thérèse (or even longer for other souls) is a mystery; the answer is different for every person. Sometimes it's because we don't really want to change. In some cases, we like our sins too much and don't want to go through all the effort to improve. In other cases, we're just scared to let go of a certain behavior that we think we can't live without; we can't imagine living any other way. While there's a part of us that "sort of" wants to change, another part of us doesn't want to let go. We're too attached to our sins. Jesus challenges us, like he did the paralyzed man in the Gospels, asking a very personal question: "Do you *want* to be healed?" (Jn 5:6, emphasis added). Jesus doesn't just want to change us; he wants us to *want* to be changed.

> "The work I had been unable to do in ten years was done by Jesus in one instant."
>
> —St. Thérèse of Lisieux

Sometimes, Jesus allows us to continue in a certain weakness because there are other areas in our souls that need more immediate attention. We might, for example, think God needs to heal us right away of our sins of impurity. But God wants us first to recognize our self-centeredness and grow in greater love for our neighbor. Or we might think we need to grow in the habit of prayer so we can meditate and contemplate as often and as well as other Christians we know. But God first wants to heal us of our vanity and pride so we don't compare ourselves to others but come to prayer as we are, willing to grow in prayer at the pace and in the manner he desires.

We also might be allowed to persist in a certain weakness so that we can grow in humility. St. Paul had a thorn in his flesh—some hidden sin that he could not overcome—because God wanted him to learn how to rely on his grace more than his own effort, to seek his help in a deeper way, and to realize that God's power was manifest through his weakness (2 Cor 12:9).

Or God might allow us to experience struggle with sins so that we grow in compassion when we notice the faults of others. Sometimes the only way we will truly learn to be patient with others' weaknesses is to come to a deeper experience of our own poverty. When we feel the weight of our own faults and experience how gentle and compassionate God is with us, we'll be more likely to respond to the shortcomings of our coworkers, neighbors, or spouses with compassion and understanding—not with critique, complaint, or condemnation.

Long-Term Healing

Finally, the process of healing might take years and decades simply because our weaknesses are so deeply engrained in our souls. Our passions, appetites, attachments, views of ourselves, views of happiness, views of our neighbor, and views of God are not easy to change. They have been etched into our souls over the course of our lifetimes. And they may take the rest of our lives to be healed.

This is something St. Augustine experiences throughout the many years after his conversion. Having lived a wild life in his youth, he eventually makes a decisive turn away from sin and surrenders his life to Jesus, becoming Catholic. He even becomes a priest, bishop, and great teacher of the Faith. But this doesn't mean he no longer struggles with sin. He may not live decadently as he did in his youth, giving

> "It's not as though I do not suffer wounds, but I feel rather that you heal them over and over again."
> —St. Augustine

in to fornication and drunkenness, or pursue the wealth, honor, and comforts of this world as the source of all his happiness. But he still struggles with impure thoughts, eating more than he needs, delighting in the praise of men, and being too attached to little luxuries, pleasures, and comforts that the world offers him. God does amazing work in his soul at his conversion, but the roots of his sins are still there. A lot more healing still needs to be done. As it was for St. Augustine, that deep healing often takes us a lifetime of ups and downs, a few steps forward and a few steps backward. And the healing is not just about overcoming a certain bad pattern of behavior or sin. It's also about healing us of the way we want to be healed: completely, right away, all at once, on our own, by our own effort. Jesus wants to heal us of that as well.

So, while we sincerely strive for holiness, we often find ourselves falling back a little into our old ways.

We experience our weaknesses, repent of our sins, and receive another dose of the medicine of Divine Mercy that strengthens us to get up and try again. We may notice a few slight improvements, but deep down we know we'll probably stumble yet another time and need his mercy once more. This is what the older Augustine describes when he is looking back over his life and says to God, "It's not as though I do not suffer wounds, but I feel rather that you heal them over and over again."[3]

What an image! God, the Divine Surgeon, needs to heal our deep wounds "over and over again." And it's through this process of being healed repeatedly that we become convinced of where the healing comes from—not from our own effort, but from God. Thérèse learns this on that Christmas Eve in 1886. And she continues to rely on God's grace throughout the rest her life. She experiences real change and comes to know in a profound way that all her acts of love are not from her alone, but from Christ working through her. "I feel it, when I am charitable, *it is Jesus alone who is acting in me.*" Jesus wants to do the same in our souls. But he can only do it if we learn to rely on his grace.

---

[3]   St. Augustine, *Confessions*, 10.39.

Reflection Questions

- How does the conversion story of St. Thérèse inspire you? Have you noticed small ways God has worked a change in your heart? Thank God for that transformation, however big or small it might be.

- Think of a weakness you've had for many years. Why do you think God has allowed you to continue in this struggle? God can bring good even out of evil. Has this weakness helped you grow in patience, trust, or humility? Has it made you more understanding and compassionate with others' faults? Has it drawn you closer to God in prayer as you pour your heart out to him for help? Or do you perhaps persist in this sin because, deep down, you don't want to give it up?

PART THREE

Transformed by Fire

Introduction to Part Three:
Keeping the Flame Burning

Some of us might remember a key moment or season in life when we first encountered Jesus "as a real living person—not just an idea," as St. Teresa of Calcutta said. Others of us might say that this realization developed gradually over a long period of time. Whatever the case may be, those initial sparks of conversion are not enough to sustain us long-term. We need to keep the flame of faith burning throughout our lives. How do we keep our relationship with Jesus growing?

The Bible underscores four key practices that mark the earliest followers of Jesus. We could think of these as the four key habits of a disciple. If we want our faith to be sustained, we need these four habits in our daily lives.

Acts 2:42 tells us that the disciples devoted themselves to:

1. The teaching of the Apostles
2. Fellowship
3. The breaking of bread
4. Prayers

While there are many creative ways one could sum up the various practices of a disciple, following the biblical model is best. When the Church has summed up the Catholic Faith, it has often turned to these four points in Acts 2:42 as a way to categorize what it means to follow Jesus. In fact, the four pillars of the *Catechism of the Catholic Church* are traditionally seen as being based on these four points.[1] So if we want a road map to help make sure we are on the right

---

[1] The four main parts of the *Catechism*—the four pillars—are as follows: the Creed (corresponding to the teaching of the Apostles); the Sacraments (corresponding to "the breaking of bread"); the moral life (corresponding to fellowship); and prayer.

track in our relationship with Jesus, we can ask ourselves if we are growing in our understanding and living out of these four basic points.

But there's more. If we want to keep the fire of faith burning, think of these four points as logs we add to the fire. The more we grow in *prayer*, in *fellowship* with other disciples, in our devotion to the *Sacraments* ("the breaking of the bread"), and in *forming our minds* with the revelation of Christ ("the Apostles' teaching"), the more we encounter Jesus ever anew. We learn something new about Christ's teachings that challenges us. We sense in prayer his inviting us to take the next step of faith. We experience his love and mercy in the Sacraments. And we are strengthened by our fellowship with other disciples who encourage us in the faith and help bring the best out of us.

We've seen how our being transformed into Christ is God's work. But these four habits help us dispose ourselves to receive the graces God wants to give us. If we want to grow as disciples and experience real healing, change, forgiveness, and love, then we want to make sure that we follow these four practices the Bible singles out as the four habits of a disciple.

The Battle for Your Mind

Right now, there's a battle going on for your mind—for how you look at reality. Who are you? What is life all about? What brings happiness? What is true success? What is love? Who is God? What happens after we die?

These are some of the most fundamental questions in life, and the world is doing everything it can to get you to look at them a certain way, while Christ offers you a very different perspective. Which outlook on life will you adopt? From the beginning of Christianity, St. Paul warned us to get ready for this battle, saying, "Do not be conformed to this world but be transformed by the renewal of your *mind*" (Rm 12:2, emphasis added).

In our modern age especially, we need to constantly put before our minds the most important truths, the highest truths, the ones that matter most. Unfortunately, many Christians who go to Mass each Sunday, pray often, and sincerely want to follow Christ are the same people who fill their minds the rest of the week with conversations, books, shows, movies, songs, images, blogs, and videos that undermine their faith. The problem is not simply that these alternative ways of looking at things such as life, love, beauty, money, or sex, for example, are coming from secular, non-Christian sources. The bigger issue is that the outlook presented by much of the secular entertainment, education, and media industries today is directly opposed to what Jesus reveals.

And we are foolishly naïve if we think it doesn't affect us.

What We Put in Our Minds Matters

What we put in our minds matters. We're made in such a way that what we put in our minds *changes us*. It shapes how we look at reality and what we perceive as good and true and beautiful. Hence, it influences our desires and what we want to pursue in life. It shapes who we become. To think that what we read, what we watch, and what we listen to doesn't affect us is simply to be out of touch with reality.

Consider, for example, how the world views romantic love. The modern world often trains us to think of love as being about *what I get out of the other person*, whether it be feelings, emotions, sensual pleasure, or a sense of not being alone. The focus is not primarily on the good of the other person, but on what that person does for me. "I love you" thus tends to mean "I get powerful feelings or a rush of emotions from you," or "I have a lot of fun with you," or "I get sexual pleasure from you." But what happens when the relationship gets challenging: when the feelings fade, the fun times go away, or your beloved can get sexual pleasure somewhere else? Will your beloved still be there for you? Deep down we know that in this kind of love the other person is not really committed to you for who you are. They're just committed to *what they get out of you*.

This view of love is very different from what Jesus reveals. Authentic love is not so self-centered. It's not about what another person does for me. True love is outward looking:

it's about seeking what's best for another person. That's how the *Catechism* defines love: "to will the good of another." Jesus models this love for us most especially on the Cross. Jesus doesn't get a lot out of being crucified on Calvary. He doesn't get a lot of warm feelings, have a fun time, or get a lot of enjoyment out of dying on the Cross. He suffers much as he gives himself completely for us. That's what real love looks like. It's about someone being truly committed to you for who you are—not for how you look, how you perform, or what you do for them.

This kind of authentic love, however, is not often portrayed in most movies, love songs, news reports, advertisements, and articles that people encounter today. That's in part why even good Christians face much confusion, disillusionment, and hurt in their dating relationships and marriages. Even though they've heard the Christian message about love, they've allowed their minds to be filled with Hollywood's version of love. Many young devout Catholics, for example, have admitted that, even though they know pre-marital sex is wrong, they still wonder if they're missing something by not having sex with their boyfriend or girlfriend because, as one young adult put it, "that's how all the beautiful love stories we see in the movies end—with the lovers in bed with each other. It makes me wonder if I'm missing out on something in my relationship."

> What we put in our minds *changes us*.

But it's not just Christian college students and young professionals who are so swayed by the culture. I've met smart, professional, successful married people in their 30s and 40s who are confused and struggling in their marriages in large part because of how they've taken in the world's view of love. I remember one Christian woman, for example, telling me, "I've been so disillusioned with my relationship with my husband these last five years because I've been wondering *why my marriage isn't turning out like all those love songs I listen to.*" Notice that her standard for love and for her marriage wasn't the Bible, Jesus, or the Church. It was the music she listens to from pop culture.

This is why we must be very careful about what we put in our minds. As Archbishop Charles Chaput has emphasized, "We need to *read*—above all the Word of God, but also history and biographies and great novels. If we don't read, we condemn ourselves to chronic stupidity and a conditioning by mass media that have no sympathy for the things we believe. Television is not a channel for serious thought. It's often just the opposite. And the Internet, for all its advantages, is too often a source of isolation. . . . If we fill our heads with poison and junk, we make ourselves angry and dumb."[1] He's certainly not saying we should never watch TV or we should avoid the Internet. But he is challenging us to be much more discerning about what we take in from the culture.

Here's one simple thing you can do to assess whether what you're filling your mind with is good or bad for your soul: Make a list of the shows, movies, music, and books you like most. Then consider what St. Paul wrote in Philippians 4:8: "Whatever is true, whatever is honorable, whatever is just, whatever is pure, whatever is lovely, whatever is gracious, if there is any excellence, if there is anything worthy of praise, think about these things." And then ask yourself if what you are taking in is true, honorable, pure, and lovely. Would you look at or listen to this if Jesus were in the room with you?

---

[1]   Archbishop Charles J. Chaput, OFM Cap., "What's Next: Catholics, America and a World Made New," *CatholicPhilly.com,* address at Napa Institute, July 27, 2017.

Highest Truths

One of the biggest challenges in our modern age is that it focuses all our attention only on this world, on what we can see. We get caught up in the pressures of life—worrying about what other people think of us, maintaining an image, building our career, making sure our kids get all the right experiences, pursuing the honors, riches, comforts, and pleasures of this world—and we become driven by the fear of missing out on what everyone else is doing. The secular environment gets us to focus on these present realities so much that we forget the spiritual realities that govern the universe and matter most in our lives.

Yet our Faith tells us the most important part of the universe is spiritual reality, which is beyond our senses: the angelic beings that surround us moment by moment, the Holy Spirit who is present to us, the life of grace in our hearts, and our own spiritual souls that will last forever. Keeping these invisible realities in mind is far more important than keeping up with what is trending on social media.

In the movie adaptation of J.R.R. Tolkien's popular novel *The Hobbit*, the main character Bilbo Baggins is on his way to fight the evil dragon Smaug on the Lonely Mountain. But to get there, he has to travel with his friends on an epic journey that involves passing through a dark forest filled with many dangers. For days, Bilbo and his companions never see the sun. The oppressively thick forest is almost asphyxiating. And when they fall off the main path, they're discouraged, not sure they're heading in the right direction and uncertain of what might come next.

But in this low moment, Bilbo decides to climb to the top of a tall tree and rise above the oppressive forest. He sees the blue sky, breathes in the fresh air, and looks all around. His perspective changes completely. He can suddenly see everything. He sees where he came from when he first entered the forest. He can get a better sense of where he is now. And, to his great delight, he can see for the first time in the distance the goal of his journey: the Lonely Mountain.

In our modern era that focuses just on this world—the honors, comforts, pursuits, and pleasures of this world— we easily lose sight of the most important realities: where we came from, where we are right now, and where we are going. Like Bilbo, we need to take the effort to climb trees—to rise above the dark forest of the secular culture that looks only at what it can see and distracts us from what's truly most important. With great effort, care, and attention, we need to raise our minds intentionally to the highest truths that God has revealed to us so that we can see our lives as they really are.[2]

The Real Story

For a moment, consider these basic but most beautiful truths: God, who was perfectly happy and glorious in himself, freely chose to create the universe to share his goodness and his love with others. But before God made the cosmos, the earth, the sky and sea, and human beings, he created the invisible universe: the angels. The angels are spiritual, non-bodily beings. Even though we can't see them, they are more powerful than anything on earth. At the dawn of creation, some of these angelic beings rebelled against God led by one of their own, named Lucifer, who must have been so very beautiful and powerful if he was able to convince other creatures to

---

[2]   I am thankful to my friend Jonathan Reyes for this analogy.

do the most foolish thing they could do: rebel against their own Creator!

These rebellious angels, known as the demons, hate God and everything God loves. When God created human beings to share in his love, Lucifer wanted to destroy this beautiful union that the human family had with God. He tempted our first parents and convinced some to join his rebellion. After that, the human family was continuously oppressed by him—until Jesus came.

God sent his Son to become one of us, to die on the Cross and liberate us from sin, death, and Satan's dominion. Satan still tries to lure us back to his ways. Because of Original Sin, we are wounded and have an inclination toward evil. Resisting temptation is still an ongoing struggle. But Christ came to restore our unity with the Father and send his Spirit into our hearts and call us to prayer, the Sacraments, and fellowship, and to form our minds in the truth so that we can follow him as disciples and not follow the ways of this world, the ways of the enemy. That's why our work of being disciples and leading others to follow Christ is, in reality, the most important thing we can do.

> Like Bilbo, we need to climb trees—to rise above the dark forest of the secular culture.

Keeping these fundamental truths at the forefront of our minds is far more important than knowing what's on the news, what videos everyone is watching, or how our favorite team is doing. It's also more important than advancing in our career, making more money, improving our golf swing, signing our kids up for summer activities, or building up our savings fund. There's nothing wrong with any of these things, but do they merit most of our attention to the point of crowding out higher spiritual truths that offer us the greatest illumination for our path in life?

Acts 2:42 reminds us that the earliest disciples of Jesus dedicated themselves to the teachings of the Apostles. And this wasn't just one of the many good things the disciples did. Forming their minds with all that Jesus revealed to the Apostles was so crucial to the original disciples that it is presented in the Bible as one of their four main practices. And it is listed *first*.

Does your life right now reflect this priority? If someone on the outside watched what you put before your mind, would that person notice you making this kind of intellectual faith formation a top priority in your life? Forming our minds is important not just for seeing clearly in a time of cultural crisis; it's essential simply for living a fully human life. For the human mind is made to rest in contemplation of what is true.

How to Form Your Mind

Now, let's get practical. What should we be doing to form our minds?

First, there are two basic texts that should be a part of the regular diet of every Catholic disciple: the Bible and the *Catechism*. We should take time to read and study the Bible, for in it we encounter God's inspired Word to us in Scripture. We also should take time to learn what's in the *Catechism of the Catholic Church*, which is the Church's official presentation of the Faith. Knowing the Bible and the *Catechism* better will help us to see reality more clearly. While some people may think of faith as a leap in the dark, we should see these two important texts as a step into the light. They help us to see things as they really are and point us toward true happiness in life. As the psalmist expresses,

"Your word is a lamp to my feet and a light to my path" (Ps 119:105).

Second, we can take time to read good books that help us contemplate and better understand prayer, the moral life, and the mysteries of faith—who God is, Jesus, the Church, the Sacraments, the Last Things. The more we learn about God and what he has revealed, the more we can give ourselves to him in love and allow his revelation to guide our lives. When we gain a deeper understanding of God's plan or a particular virtue or a truth we hadn't grasped before, it challenges us to live according to that truth more. Or it may inspire us to praise God for his goodness, to thank him for his blessings, or to ask his forgiveness for not living according to his plan in this way.

Third, we can form our minds by participating in a Bible study or other small faith formation group at our parish. We can attend presentations, retreats, and conferences. We can also listen to good Catholic radio and podcasts, read Catholic blogs, follow videos, and hear Catholic speakers. But here we must be careful. We can certainly be enriched by listening to podcasts while driving, cooking, or folding laundry, or by viewing an occasional inspirational quote, short video, or link to a blog article from someone's social media post. But we want to keep two things in mind when using new media even for good Catholic content: its power to distract us and its limitations in forming our minds well.

"Look Down! Look Down!"

The blockbuster film musical *Les Misérables* opens with a dramatic scene: hundreds of French convicts pulling dozens of ropes to bring a massive ship into harbor. Armed French soldiers walk up and down the rows of prisoners making sure not a single person slacks for a moment. Condemned to this slave-like labor as part of their punishment, the prisoners pull with all their might and avoid eye contact with the officers, singing to each other the musical's opening song, "Look down...Look down!"

Today a similar form of slavery is emerging. But it's one we bring upon ourselves. Many people fill their days moving from one click to the next on their phones, checking messages, updates, emails, posts, and links. In between meetings. While waiting in line. When at the park with their kids. What does everyone do in these moments? They *look down* at their phones. They have no time to think. To sit in quiet. To plan their days. They move from one alert to the next, governed by their phones and not their minds.

Even devout Catholics are susceptible to this. On the outside, they may look very Catholic. They might go to Mass, visit the chapel, and say some prayers at certain moments, but the rest of their days are filled with one media distraction after another. And just because the media they're consuming is often Catholic, that doesn't mean it's all good for their souls. The sheer amount of time one can spend with media and its power of distraction can inhibit our intellects, keeping our minds bouncing from one thing to the next, hindering us from concentrating well, thinking clearly, contemplating truth, and hearing the voice of God.

People today have little space interiorly for silence. Contemplation. Thought. Yet God speaks to us in silence; if we don't fight for silence in our lives, we will be slaves to the incessant, distracting, indeed demanding noise all around us. Instead of looking down at our phones throughout the day, let's virtuously set parameters around when and how much we use them. Let's keep them more at bay so we can live a fuller human life and *look up* to the higher things in life, whether it's creating space to think about what's most important each day or literally looking up and gazing at the people in our lives. If we do, we'll find ourselves giving more of our attention to our actual children, spouses, friends, and God—and not just what Catholic media says *about* them.

Reading a Good Book

No podcast, radio show, or newsfeed can replace the impact of reading a good book. Again, good Catholic content delivered through modern media forms can certainly enrich our lives. I've personally been involved in helping produce a number of these kinds of programs, and I know people whose lives have been changed by what they've taken in from a podcast, a video, a TV show, or a recorded talk. But when it comes to the kind of faith formation you need as a disciple who is not "conformed to this world" but is being "transformed by the renewal of [your mind]," it's not enough. We need more than a show or blog can offer, which is why the best of Catholic media outlets don't see themselves as the ultimate solution, but point their audiences to the deeper sources that are able to *form our minds* with the wisdom of God.

Remember the quote from Archbishop Chaput earlier in this chapter: "We need to *read*" the Word of God and the great books. Through modern media, we can certainly have moments of learning some new information ("I never knew about that saint") or a deeper understanding of a certain truth ("That helped me understand this aspect of the Faith I always had questions about") or being inspired in a certain way ("I needed to hear that—this will help my prayer life!"). And that is all great. But modern media shouldn't replace the formation we could receive from reading a good book—whether that book is the Bible, the *Catechism*, a classic from the Catholic tradition, or a book from the great teachers of our day. After all, being filled with a lot of good information, even if it is Christian, does not make one holy, and knowing a lot of different facts, even if they are Catholic facts, does not make one wise. As T. S. Eliot once wrote,

> Where is the wisdom we have lost in
>   knowledge?
> Where is the knowledge we have lost in
>   information?[3]

If you find enrichment from the information found in good Catholic blogs, podcasts, YouTube videos, and radio shows, keep using them! Just make sure you are also feeding your mind with good books, classes, and other experiences that form your intellect with a clear, orderly presentation of the Faith. Good books, courses, and faith formation programs can do much more to form one's mind than a show or blog can ever hope to accomplish.

Of course, if we want to be wise and have the truths of the Faith sink in, shape us, and indeed, become a part of us, we need time to reflect. Important truths are like seeds in that they need time to take root in our minds. And when they take root, they help us see reality correctly and can serve to guide our lives. As St. Thomas Aquinas explains, "To understand, it is necessary that those things that a man hears become, as it were, connatural to him in order that they may be impressed perfectly on his mind. For

---

[3] T. S. Eliot, "Choruses from 'The Rock,'" in *The Complete Poems and Plays: 1909–1950* (Orlando: Harcourt Brace & Company, 1971), 96–116.

this a man needs time in which his intellect may be confirmed in what it has received, by much meditation."[4]

You may have had the experience of reading a paragraph from a good article or book that was so insightful that you put it down for a moment and took time to think about the point the author was making.

> Our phones are not built for contemplation.

You pondered for a few moments its meaning and significance. If someone were to ask you later about what you were reading, you'd be able to say something thoughtful about it because you internalized the truth you encountered.

But you may also have had the experience of reading something quickly, superficially, on-the-go as you raced to the next thing. You remember liking what you read, but you would not be able to articulate one important point from the piece in a coherent way.

There are many things we come across in the media that do not require our meditating on them. For these, a quick glance, a superficial read, a passive listening to something in the background is just fine. I don't need to contemplate, for example, the highlights of my favorite team's game, my friend's post about his vacation, or the weather report I'm hearing on the radio. Even much content in Catholic media—interviews, shows, posts—don't require the mind's full attention. We might consider them simply as wholesome entertainment, maybe even inspiring or motivational. But let's not confuse that with serious faith formation. If we want the most important truths of our Faith to take

---

[4] St. Thomas Aquinas, *Commentary on Aristotle's Nicomachean Ethics*, trans. C. I. Litzinger, OP (Notre Dame, Indiana: Dumb Ox Books, 1993), no. 1344. I am grateful to my colleague Chris Blum for the seed analogy and for his pointing me to this insight from Aquinas.

root in our soul, we need to take time to contemplate them. And time for meditating on truth is precisely what's missing in most of our media consumption.

Our phones, for example, are not built for such contemplation. They are intentionally designed to keep us moving rapidly from one click to the next. We might fill our minds with incessant scattered images, sounds, words, and messages on a screen, but even when we encounter a truth in a video, article, show, or post, how often do we put the phone down and take time to contemplate it—to mull it over in our minds, try to understand it better, and ponder its significance so it takes root in our souls?

> But don't think the battle is just about the kind of *content* you take in. Today, the battle is also about *the way* you take it in.

And this leads to a final point: we need to be honest and ask ourselves how much of our media use, even when it's Catholic media, is more about entertainment and distraction than it is about real faith formation. To help us discern our Catholic media use, we should ask ourselves whether we're using this media primarily to consume it—like a tasty piece of pizza—or to foster a thoughtful pondering of what's true in a way that leads to an encounter with Jesus Christ, who is Truth. There's nothing wrong with eating a piece of pizza, but we should examine whether we're often turning to our phones or screens primarily to satisfy a craving (hoping just one more click will give us some psychological reward), to entertain ourselves, to fill a void because we don't like silence and being alone with our own thoughts, or to create a feeling of staying "connected" because we fear missing out on what everyone else is doing.

From the beginning, there has been a battle for our minds. But don't think the battle is just about the kind of content you take in (Is it Catholic? Or is it R-rated material?). Today, the battle is also about the way you take it in. For the new kinds of media themselves—their power to distract, their lure in taking up so much of our time, their tendency to keep us at the superficial and train our minds to avoid deeper, serious thought—are intentionally designed in a way that keeps us from contemplation. We should seriously weigh the amount and manner in which we use the new media.

Reflection Questions

- St. Paul writes, "Do not be conformed to this world, but be transformed by the renewal of your mind" (Rom 12:2). In what ways does your mind sometimes conform to the standards of this world—its view of love, beauty, and success; its pursuit of wealth, comfort, pleasure, and the praise of men; its tendency to focus only on visible realities and this present world? What can you do to combat these tendencies and form your mind in the truth so that you see reality more clearly?

- Take a moment to examine your use of media. Are there shows, videos, songs, or images you take in that do not follow God's standards for what is true, good, pure, and beautiful? Do you spend too much time on screens, with your phone, with noise constantly distracting you? What can you do to build more silence into your soul, to reflect on truth and hear the voice of God?

Christian Friendship

If we want to keep the fire of faith burning, there's a second practice we need to incorporate into our lives that's absolutely crucial: fellowship with other disciples. We can't expect to grow in our relationship with Christ on our own. We need other brothers and sisters who are running beside us—and I mean *running*. They're not just Christians in name or churchgoers who are passively going through the motions with their faith. Like you, they have inside them that spark of a disciple who is intentionally running after Christ, striving for a deeper union with him. Do you have some friendships like this—friendships with other disciples who are seeking Christ's will for their lives, pursuing prayer, virtue, and holiness, earnestly struggling to be more and more like Jesus in all areas of their lives?

The Bible says that "iron sharpens iron, and one man sharpens another" (Prv 27:17). An iron blade cannot be made razor-sharp by a dull one. It takes one sharp blade to sharpen another. Similarly, we need fellow disciples in our lives so we can be sharpened by their own example and pursuit of Christ. So important is Christian fellowship in the life of a disciple that the Acts of the Apostles lists it as one of the four key practices to which Jesus's earliest followers devoted themselves (see Acts 2:42).

Getting Some *Haverim*

In the Judaism of Jesus's day, disciples didn't just have a rabbi to mentor them. They had each other. Their formation wasn't just about a one-on-one relationship between a disciple and his rabbi. Biblical discipleship wasn't as individualistic as our modern "me and Jesus" or "I'm spiritual but don't need a church" attitudes tend to be. Rather, a disciple was immersed in a community with fellow disciples, friends (called *haverim* in Hebrew) who were striving for a common goal and helping each other to get there. Together, they learned from their master's teachings and example. They wrestled together over the same sacred texts. They discussed, debated, and challenged each other. They honored, supported, and encouraged each other. Most of all, they pushed each other. Being surrounded by *haverim*, others who had thrown their entire lives into taking on the ways of their rabbi, made each individual disciple better.[1]

"Iron sharpens iron, and one man sharpens another." (Prv 27:17)

Growing up playing soccer, one of my sons was used to being one of the best players on his little recreational team. Playing with others who were just playing for fun, he stood out for his intensity and passion about the game, his hard work at practice, and his dribbling and passing skills. But as he moved into his teen years and began playing competitive club soccer, things were more challenging. He was no longer the top player on the team. There were many who were bigger, stronger, faster, more skilled, or

---

[1]   Though the word itself means a close friend or companion, in the context of rabbi-disciple relationships, it can point to the fellowship of disciples learning together.

more confident. He didn't score as many goals as he used to. And he certainly didn't stand out on the team. But he was being pushed. Now he was immersed in a group with others who were just as serious and committed to improving as he was. Playing week in and week out with others whose touch with the ball, power of shot, speed of play, and understanding of the game was just as good as his or even better rubbed off on him and challenged him to give his best in a way he never could have if he had remained the standout kid in recreational soccer. The other players brought out the best in him.

At what level are you pushing yourself in your walk with the Lord? Do you sit back and say, "Well, I've got some good friends. They may not be as devout in their faith, but they're decent people. I don't need anything else." Or do you intentionally seek to have other committed disciples—some *haverim*—in your life who bring the best out of you?

Here we must be clear: Christian fellowship is not just about having a friend who happens to be Catholic. It's also much more than being surrounded by mere "fans" of the Catholic Faith—people outwardly orthodox and excited but not inwardly striving for virtue and sanctity. It's about having others beside you who are running after Christ as a disciple like you are: *haverim*. They are wrestling with God's Word and the teachings of the Church, striving to understand them better and apply them to their lives. As one author put it, it's like having a "spiritual jogging partner—someone for whom you'll crawl out of bed on a rainy morning, putting on your running shoes instead of hitting the snooze button. Once you're up and running together, your pace is a little faster, you keep going a little longer. You are pushed intellectually and spiritually. If we really want to mature in faith and as disciples, we need to develop relationships that force us to grow, by getting ourselves some *haverim*."[2]

A good way to discern whether you have *haverim* is to consider what you tend to talk about with your friends. Do your conversations remain at the level of office gossip, sports, politics, movie lines, the latest episode of some popular show, your exciting vacation, and the accomplishments of your children last week? Or do you have close friends with whom you can rise above the trivial and from time to time talk about the things that matter most in life—God, prayer, virtue, living marriage well, building strong families? Do you have close friends with whom you can share your struggles in living out your Catholic Faith, in growing in your relationship with God? Do you have friends with whom you can discuss how to overcome bad habits and sin or challenges in your dating, marriage, or family relationships, and find encouragement and good advice?

Keep the Fire Burning

When making a charcoal fire, it's best to put all the coals together in one pile so that they feed off each other's heat. Together, each coal will burn stronger and longer than if it were isolated from the others. But what happens when one coal is separated from the other burning coals? It won't burn as strongly, and it will soon die out.

The same thing happens when a disciple doesn't have fellowship with other committed disciples. When we don't

---

[2] Lois Tverberg, *Walking in the Dust of Rabbi Jesus* (Grand Rapids: Zondervan, 2012), 74.

have *haverim* in our lives, our growth as disciples is more likely to be stunted. We may even fall back into old bad habits or turn away from true discipleship, settling for mediocrity in our faith.

Especially in a secular culture that is constantly luring us away from Christian values, we need brothers and sisters who are part of our lives to help keep us on track, reminding us that we're not alone in our pursuit of Christ and that the effort and sacrifices we make in our total commitment to him are worth it. Our secular world is not going to offer that kind of encouragement. Quite the opposite. The world presents its many attractive honors, comforts, riches, shows, entertainments, pleasures, and pursuits as the fun and exciting kind of life. Meanwhile, Christian ideals like chastity, honesty, sacrifice, appreciating the blessing of children, living simply, serving the poor, and having faith in a God we cannot see seem hard, difficult, and boring. Why would anyone want to live like that?

Do you have close friends with whom you can rise above the trivial and talk about the things that matter most in life?

If we're surrounded by people who don't share these values with the same intensity as we do or don't share them at all, we become like that isolated coal. Our flame of faith is not likely to grow and may be at a greater risk of dying out. We can certainly have friendships with people of different backgrounds. But having some regular fellowship with others who share our conviction in Christ is crucial. We need to live in joyful fellowship with other *disciples who are striving after the same Christian ideals*. We need to have regular contact with the other burning coals. It helps keep us on track, strengthens us in our most noble pursuits, makes us better, sharpens our swords, and continually re-enkindles the fire of our faith.

Where to Find Fellowship

True Christian friendships like these are vital for our walk with the Lord, but can sometimes be hard to find. If we don't know people in our area who are on fire with their faith, the first thing we should do is pray for fellowship. We should bring that desire to the Lord, for he wants this for us and is with us in our search for good Christian friendships.

We also may want to turn to a nearby parish to look for opportunities for smaller groups of believers who get together on a regular basis to learn more about living the faith and be enriched by each other's experiences. Some are based on people's state in life, such as various men's and women's groups, groups for married couples, groups for single people, moms' groups, groups for fathers, or young adult groups. Other small groups are more centered on particular interests: some gather to study the Bible, some are based on learning more about the Church's teachings and how to explain them, and some are service-oriented, dedicated to various projects at the parish or serving the poor in the local community. Some just gather for meals, fellowship, and prayer. If you don't already have some devout Catholic friends who are running after Christ, small groups at your parish or in your diocese may be a helpful option to pursue.

Encountering Christ in Our Neighbor

Finally, while fellowship helps build us up in the faith, it also is a school of self-giving. We learn to show our love for Christ by loving Jesus in our neighbors.

That's an important lesson St. Catherine of Siena once learned. After spending a few years in almost complete silence and solitude in prayer with the Lord, she heard God ask her to go back out into the world and live in fellowship with others. She was nervous about this, afraid that she would lose the intimacy she was experiencing with God in solitude. But God told her that she needed to learn to walk on two feet—both love of God and love of neighbor.

We don't want to be one-legged Christians who hop on the single leg of "loving God," while neglecting the other leg of "loving neighbor." For holiness does not consist in how many rosaries one recites, how many hours one prays in the chapel, or how smart one becomes in knowledge of the faith. According to many saints, a major sign of someone's growing in holiness is his or her growing in patient, gentle, generous, merciful love of neighbor. Indeed, we grow in love of Christ through learning to love our neighbor—whether it be a spouse, coworker, relative, or friend—with all their quirks, needs, weaknesses, and faults. In so doing, we are simply learning to love others the way God loves us—freely, patiently, mercifully, and unconditionally, expecting nothing back. This is especially true in regard to those in most need: the poor. When we grow in sacrificial love for the poor—whether the materially poor or the many spiritually poor around us—we come to a deeper encounter with the Lord himself. Indeed, care for the poor is an essential part of what it means to be a disciple. As Jesus teaches, "Truly, I say to you, as you did it to one of the least of these my brethren, you did it to me" (Mt 25:40).

> God told her that she needed to learn to walk on two feet—both love of God and love of neighbor.

Reflection Questions

- What's the difference between authentic Christian fellowship (having *haverim*) and just ordinary friends who happen to be Christian in name? Why is it important to have true fellowship? What can you do to make Christian fellowship more of a priority in your life?

- Consider your close Christian friends who are "burning coals" in your life. How have they shaped you? How do they help you grow as a disciple? Take a moment to thank God for them.

Amazing Signs, Amazing Grace

If you want to be healed of your wounds and imperfections, then you want to go to the Sacraments. If you want to overcome your sins and grow in the spiritual life, then go to the Sacraments as often as you can. If you want better friendships, a stronger marriage, a better family life, or a deeper understanding of God's plan for you, the graces unleashed in the Sacraments can help you. Most of all, if you want to become more like Jesus and encounter him regularly in the way he most directly wants to transform you, then go to the Sacraments.

The Sacraments are not simply the rituals we have to perform to be good Christians or hoops we have to jump through because we happen to be Catholic. Rather, the Sacraments are the most amazing events taking place every day in the whole world! They aren't random rituals from our religion, but gifts given to us by Our Lord Jesus so we can encounter him, the living God, today. Jesus himself established the Sacraments, entrusting the graces of salvation to the Church, so they can be unleashed through these seven sacred acts. Through the Sacraments, Jesus takes the treasures he won for us on the Cross some 2,000 years ago and applies them to our lives now. It's where he does his most profound work in our souls, turning sinners into saints one small step at a time.

Most of the Sacraments either are received only one time (Baptism, Confirmation) or, if they can be received more than once, are received rarely (the Anointing of the Sick, Matrimony, Holy Orders). But there are two Sacraments we can receive frequently throughout our lives: Reconciliation and the Eucharist. Let's take a look at how a disciple encounters Jesus in these two Sacraments on a regular basis.

Confession

The Sacrament of Reconciliation brings us right into the heart of our discipleship. As disciples of Jesus, we strive to imitate him and root out sin in our lives. But we always come up short and experience our own weaknesses and our inability to change. As we saw in chapter six, this is precisely where God wants to meet us with his love: in the truth of who we are, in the valley of humility. And there is no more profound encounter with God's mercy than in the Sacrament of Reconciliation. Let's consider the two amazing things that happen in Confession.

First, we are freed. God wants to free us of our sins and all the uneasiness, guilt, or shame we might experience over what we have done. When we are truly sorry for our sins, God sees our contrite hearts. He is not sitting back angry, pointing his finger, and condemning us for our sins. Rather, he's like the father racing out to meet his prodigal son. Love makes him want to remove whatever obstacles keep him from being reunited with his son. That's the God we meet in Confession. And how liberating it is to hear the priest tell us that our sins really are forgiven! "I absolve you of your sins."

So, no matter what you've done, no matter how many times you've done it, and no matter how long you've been away from Confession, know that Jesus is waiting for you in the Sacrament of Reconciliation. He longs to lift the burden of your sins and give you a new start in life.

Strength for the Battle

But that's not all. There's a second amazing thing Jesus wants to do in our souls through Confession. Jesus doesn't just want to forgive us. He wants to *heal* us. As I mentioned in chapter eight, God doesn't just want to pardon us like a judge. He wants to get to the roots of our sins and cure us of our spiritual illnesses and wounds. He wants us to experience real change. In the Sacrament of Reconciliation, God gives us graces to avoid those sins in the future. We receive "an increase of spiritual strength for the Christian battle."[1]

This is amazing! This is one of the main reasons we want to go to Confession regularly. If we want to grow as disciples— if we want to access Christ's power to heal our weaknesses, overcome bad habits, and avoid falling into the same sins in the future—we should go to Confession as much as possible.

Too often, however, we treat Confession like the dry cleaner. When I get a stain on my shirt, I take it to the dry cleaner. The dry cleaner removes the stain, and the shirt looks like new again. Sometimes we can approach Confession this way: we take our sins to Confession where God removes the stain of our sin and we are forgiven. But our sins are not merely a stain on our soul that needs to be wiped away. Our sins leave us with a deep wound. They forge bad habits. They form patterns of living that make it difficult for us to love

---

[1]   *CCC*, 1496.

God fully. Jesus wants to get to *the roots* of our sins and heal those deeper wounds.[2]

Now let's turn to the second Sacrament a disciple receives frequently: the Eucharist.

The Eucharist: Three Ways to Deepen Your Devotion

Do you ever feel like you're just going through the motions at Mass? You stand up, sit down, and kneel when you're supposed to. You say, "Amen," "Alleluia," and "Thanks be to God" on cue with everyone else. You're going through the motions but your mind is wandering and your heart is not fully in it. An hour goes by and you wonder if you got anything out of Mass.

Don't let that discourage you. Remember that the words you recite and the actions you perform at Mass are themselves good and holy. By simply showing up at Mass, saying the sacred prayers, and worthily receiving Jesus in Holy Communion, you are giving something beautiful to God. And you're receiving something beautiful from him—his very Body and Blood!—even if your participation is far from perfect. So if you come with a sincere desire to give God your best, and in the end you're distracted or feel you weren't as into it as you wish, give God your broken, imperfect gift and tell him you'll try to do better next time.

At the same time, we want to improve. A true disciple doesn't want to just go through the motions. We want to encounter Jesus more profoundly in the liturgy and allow the graces of this supreme gift to bear much fruit in our souls. Here are three simple things we can do to increase our devotion to Jesus in the Eucharist.

---

[2] Pope Francis, *The Name of God is Mercy* (New York: Image, 2016), 26.

Do You Prepare for Mass?—Encountering the Word

First, *prepare yourself to encounter Jesus in the Liturgy of the Word*. In the Mass, God wants to speak to us through the readings from Scripture. These are not just stories from a long time ago or an instruction book on how to live a good life. The Bible doesn't just speak *about* God. It is *God's own words to us* in the words of men. Since these are God's words, they can tran-
scend time and speak directly to us today. Indeed, the same Holy Spirit who inspired the

> Jesus wants to get to *the roots* of our sins and heal those deeper wounds.

words of Scripture some 2,000 years ago and more is alive in our hearts today, prompting us to apply those words to our lives. Indeed, at Mass, the proclamation of the Word is not merely a reading for the whole congregation. It's a *personal* word from God spoken to each individual. It's meant to comfort, encourage, or challenge each disciple in his or her particular situation at that moment. That's why people attending the same Mass can be touched by the same readings in very different ways. Someone might sense God calling him to grow in a certain virtue. Another person might take away a much-needed word of encouragement for a challenge she's facing in her family. And still another person might find the reading shedding light on an important decision he has to make.

Vatican II taught that "in the sacred books, the Father who is in heaven meets His children with great love and speaks with them."[3] But are we ready to listen to him at each Mass? Do we prayerfully enter into dialogue with

---

[3] Vatican II, Dogmatic Constitution on Divine Revelation *Dei verbum* (November 18, 1965), no. 21.

God when we hear the readings? To get ready for this powerful encounter with God's Word, we need to prepare. When the Israelites are about to hear God's Word spoken to them at Mount Sinai, they take this moment so seriously that they prepare for it by consecrating themselves to the Lord for three days. Meanwhile, many of us drive to our churches making phone calls, listening to podcasts, or talking about our team's chances in the football game that afternoon. We stumble into Mass just in time for the opening hymn and somehow expect God's Word to penetrate our hearts.

There are some simple things we can do to enhance our encounter with God's Word and spiritually transition ourselves for this sacred moment. We can turn off the noise, if even for just the last five minutes of the drive. We can say some prayers as we're driving in, such as a decade of the Rosary. Some families read the Mass readings together in the car on the way to church and talk about them. Other people try to show up five or ten minutes early to Mass to have time to quiet their souls, pray to God, or even pull out the missalettes in their pews and prayerfully review the readings before the liturgy begins. These are just suggestions. But we should all do something to prepare. To get more out of the Liturgy of the Word, we need to put something into it.

Holy Communion: Make a Thanksgiving

A second thing we can do at Mass is take time for thanksgiving after receiving the Eucharist.

As disciples, we're called to imitate our Rabbi, Jesus Christ. But we've seen how, unlike other rabbis, Jesus doesn't merely offer us an example to observe from the outside. He actually abides within us! And he does this most profoundly when we've received him in Holy Communion.

But, to appreciate this great gift, let's make sure we understand the mystery of the Eucharist clearly. The Eucharist is not just a symbol of Jesus or a reminder of his love for us. At the words of consecration, the bread and wine are actually changed. They are no longer bread and wine, but are changed into the Body and Blood of Christ. This is not a chemical change. If you put a consecrated host under a microscope, you would not suddenly see Jesus's blood cells, body tissue, or bones. All the outward sensible appearances of bread and wine remain. But under those outward appearances, Jesus's Body, Blood, Soul, and Divinity are truly present.

So, when we receive Holy Communion, we are receiving Christ himself into our souls. Think about what this means: Our God loves us so much that he comes to us at every Mass under the appearance of bread and wine and then enters into us at Holy Communion! *This is the most profound union we can have with our God here on earth.* Do we take this moment seriously? We become like the Temple that housed God's presence in Jerusalem. We become like the Blessed Virgin Mary who carried Jesus in her womb. Our God is dwelling within us sacramentally in Holy Communion!

When we come back to our pews after receiving Holy Communion, it is not the time to look around and see who's at Mass, or daydream about the football game in the afternoon, or develop our "parking lot exit strategy." And it's certainly not appropriate to leave before Mass is over. This is the most intimate time we have with our God—to talk to him from the depths of our hearts. As he is lovingly dwelling within us, we should use these profound moments to tell him we love him, to thank him for the blessings in our lives, to pour out our hearts to him with whatever may be troubling us, and to quietly rest in his love and listen to him. This is the traditional practice of making "thanksgiving" after receiving the Eucharist. We can take this time right after we receive

> We become like the Blessed Virgin Mary who carried Jesus in her womb.

Communion and return to our pews. We might even stay after Mass for a few minutes to rest quietly with Jesus before rushing off to say hello to friends, grab a donut, or race to the car. We should let those intimate moments linger as long as we can. If we don't take time to enter into dialogue with God while he is dwelling within us in Holy Communion, when will we ever really talk to him?

Making a Visit

Imagine if it were announced that some famous person you admired—your sports hero, your favorite author, or the pope—was coming to your town today and wanted to meet you individually. Surely you would do whatever you could to make time to meet this person! Now imagine if Jesus were coming to your town and wanted to meet with you. What true believer wouldn't make it a priority to take the opportunity to visit with him? Yet that's what's really happening at every Catholic parish where the Eucharist resides. Indeed, consecrated Eucharistic Hosts are given such special reverence in the Church that they are placed in a sacred space called a Tabernacle that has a candle next to it, reminding us that God is truly present there.

And this leads to a third way that disciples can deepen their devotion to the Eucharist: by taking time to visit Jesus in the Blessed Sacrament.

Love longs to be near the beloved. And our God loves us so much he wants to remain close to us, to be available to us always. That's why he remains present to us in all the Tabernacles throughout the world. The same Jesus who walked the streets of Palestine, comforting the suffering, healing the sick, raising the dead, and calling people to repent—that same Jesus is sacramentally present to us in our parishes, longing to bring guidance, healing, and change to our lives. He's just waiting for us to take time to visit him.

That's why many disciples make it a priority to stop by a Catholic church or Eucharistic chapel where the Blessed Sacrament resides. They walk in, genuflect, and draw near to their God who is really present there. They gaze at the Tabernacle and talk to Jesus. They praise him, thank him, adore him, beg him for help, seek his guidance, or just rest in his holy presence. As St. Josemaría Escrivá said, the Eucharist is "God waiting for us, God who loves man, who searches us out, who loves us just as we are—limited, selfish, inconstant, but capable of discovering his infinite affection and of giving ourselves fully to him."[4]

We certainly can pray to God anywhere—at home, in a park, in the car, or in the office. But in our Catholic churches and Eucharistic chapels, Jesus is substantially present to us in a unique way: Body, Blood, Soul, and Divinity. We approach God most profoundly. He's there for us if we want to pour our hearts out to him in need or just talk to him as a friend. Even simply sitting in his holy presence does something profound for us. It's like sitting in the sun. You don't have to do anything, but simply

---

[4] St. Josemaría Escrivá, *Christ is Passing By* (New York: Scepter, 1974), 344.

allowing the sun's rays to shine on you changes your skin color—you get a tan. Similarly, simply basking in God's presence in the Eucharist slowly changes us. We find a deeper peace, a new perspective, and a comfort in simply having a place to turn. Most of all, the more we allow the Son of God to shine on us through his Real Presence in the Eucharist, the more his love radiates through us and we become like the one we love. As Pope St. John Paul II once said, "Jesus awaits us in this sacrament of love. Let us be generous with our time in going to meet Him in adoration and in contemplation that is full of faith.... Let our adoration never cease."[5]

Reflection Questions

- What can you do to increase devotion to the Eucharist? Do you need to spiritually prepare for Mass more? Do you take time to talk to God and rest in his presence after receiving Holy Communion? Do you ever make a visit to the Blessed Sacrament outside of Mass?

- What keeps you from going to Confession more regularly or going at all? If you're afraid to go, tell Jesus your fears. If you're too busy, tell Jesus your desire to go and ask him to open up an opportunity for that to happen—and then be on the lookout for God opening that door!

---

[5] Pope St. John Paul II, apostolic letter *Dominicae Cenae* (February 24, 1980), no. 3.

The Primacy of the Interior Life

Do you set aside time each day for this most fundamental practice of a disciple—daily prayer? And by that, I mean more than simply saying a few prayers each day like the Our Father or Hail Mary or grace before meals. I also refer to more than doing various devotions such as the Rosary or Chaplet of Divine Mercy. The daily prayer life of a disciple involves even more than the highest form of prayer, participating in the Mass.

If we want to be disciples who follow Jesus, we must have at the heartbeat of our spiritual life a daily encounter with him that the Church has called "meditation"—time for reflecting on Christ's life and intimate conversation with God about how his life speaks to us today and how we can live like him more. All those other forms of prayer certainly help deepen the spiritual life. But they might only be fruitful to the extent that those vocal prayers, devotions, and graces from the Sacraments meet the fertile soil of a daily encounter with Jesus in meditative prayer.

Radiating Christ or Just Yourself?

A lot is riding on our commitment to daily prayer. First of all, our relationship with God depends on it!

Some souls wonder why their spiritual life seems stagnant. They believe in God. They say their various prayers and devotions. They go to Mass. "Why am I not growing in fervor? Why am I still struggling with certain sins? Why am I not growing in holiness?" There can be many reasons for a stalled discipleship, but one might be the lack of a commitment to daily meditation and contemplation.

But it's not just our own spiritual lives at stake. Other people's lives are impacted by our faithfulness to daily prayer. When we fail to live deeply, cultivating our interior lives, we live more superficially—relying on our own abilities, gifts, talents, personality, and effort more than on God's grace.

> "Let them look up and see no longer me but only Jesus."
> —Prayer of St. Teresa of Calcutta

God, of course, wants to use our abilities, but even more than that, he wants us to be a channel of his love to the world. So my prayer life isn't just for me. My wife and children, for example, need me to pray. They need a lot more than my love for them. For, as sincere and noble as it might be, my love is far from perfect. It's tainted by pride, impatience, fears, and wounds. My family needs Christ's love working through me.

Similarly, the people we encounter in the office, at the parish, and in our friendships need a lot more than a charming personality, hard work, organizational skills, or intelligent insights. They need Jesus radiating through us. When we live deeply, from our interior lives, we can give our missions, our jobs, our families, and our world something much greater than ourselves. We can give Christ. A prayer St. Teresa of Calcutta had her Missionary of Charity sisters recite each day sums up well the attitude of a disciple who is committed to daily prayer: "Shine through me and be so in me that every soul I come in contact with may feel Your presence in my soul. Let them look up and see no longer me but only Jesus."[1]

The Power of Meditation

For some, however, the word *meditation* might sound intimidating: very complex and only for advanced disciples. We might envision a monk or some mystic sitting with legs crossed, eyes closed, breathing slowly, and communing with God for several hours straight. "I'm just a beginner. I can barely sit still for five minutes. I'm not ready for those higher forms of prayer yet!" But meditation in the life of ordinary Christians is not that complicated. If you're a believer who loves God and can read, think, and prayerfully reflect on what you're reading, you can do basic meditative prayer. The *Catechism* describes meditation simply in this way: "The mind seeks to understand the why and how of the Christian life, in order to adhere and respond to what the Lord is asking."[2]

You can do meditation anywhere: at a church, in a chapel, at home, in your office, on the plane, in a rocking chair while holding a baby. Pope St. John Paul II even thought subways in Paris could be places for meditation and contemplation. And we can do it any time. While mornings are often recommended (so that we start our day with prayer), many disciples pray at their lunch break, after work, or in the evening before they go to bed.

---

[1] Adapted from Blessed John Henry Newman, "Jesus, the Light of the Soul," in *Everyday Meditations* (Manchester, NH: Sophia Institute Press, 2013), 85–87. St. Teresa of Calcutta greatly admired Newman's prayer, and she had the Missionary of Charity sisters pray an adapted version.

[2] *CCC*, 2705.

Most importantly, though meditation demands hard work and commitment, the practice itself is fairly simple. You just need a sacred text like the Bible, the writing of a saint, a classical spiritual book like *The Imitation of Christ*, or short reflections in modern resources such as *Magnificat* or *Our Daily Bread*. You read a few lines, a few sentences, or even just a few words. If it's a passage from the Gospels, for example, you might put yourself in the scene, imagining the sights, sounds, and smells, what Jesus says, how people respond, and how you would feel if he approached you in this scene. If it's a spiritual book, you might ponder a particular insight, pausing at parts that grab your attention or speak to what you're going through in your life now. Whether from Scripture or the Catholic tradition, the sacred text feeds our prayer. It gives us something to chew on, so to speak. It helps us to ponder God and different aspects of the Christian life and gives us a talking point for our conversation with God. It fosters an encounter with God through his inspired Word and his Church.

But it's important to note how meditation is not merely spiritual reading. Christians might be tempted to turn their prayer time into study hall and fail to enter into dialogue with God. We should talk to God about what we are reading and pondering. We ask the Lord how a certain point might apply to our lives and how he might be speaking to us through that insight. We also ask God to help us live it out. We should sit quietly and listen, trying to be aware of the ways the Lord might be stirring our hearts, nudging us, comforting us, or encouraging us. In the process, we may find ourselves, for example, moved to praise and thank the Lord for his goodness. We might gain some fresh insight on a certain problem or decision we're facing. We may find a particular point offering us much needed encouragement. Or we might sense God is calling us to repent of something: to turn away from a certain sin, to express sorrow for our actions, or to recommit ourselves to following Jesus more fully.

Resolution

Whatever inspiration flows out of our meditation, we should always conclude with a resolution—a concrete action item that helps us to follow God's promptings and put the fruit of our meditation into practice that day. For example, after meditating on Jesus's words "Be not afraid," we might make a resolution to confidently entrust whatever difficulties we'll face this day to the Lord. Or after pondering Jesus's compassion for the sick, we might make a resolution to go out of our way to be kind to people we know who are going through difficult times or to pray for those people we know who are ill.

A resolution can consist of an act of kindness. (I will praise three people today; I will thank each of my family members for something; I will offer to help someone at work.) It could be a small sacrifice. (I'm going to give up dessert; I'm going to give in to others' preferences today.) It might involve a change in behavior. (I'm not going to watch that show anymore; I'm not going to lose my temper today; I'm not going to look at my phone after dinner.) Or it could be simply remembering

Christians might be tempted to turn their prayer time into study hall.

something from your meditation (God's mercy, the peace Jesus promises us, his compassion for the suffering, his admonition not to judge other people). The kinds of resolutions will vary from person to person and day to day. The resolution is a way for the movement in your soul during meditation to bear fruit in your life; it helps you take the promptings or insights God placed on your soul and apply them to your life that day.

Using our prayer time to merely ponder spiritual insights without a resolution, however, can have its dangers. St. Francis de Sales explains that our hearts can be stirred when pondering a profound insight about the spiritual life. We are filled with joy, love, excitement, and fervor. But if we don't gather those movements in our souls into concrete plans to apply them to our lives, then correcting our faults and imitating Christ will be a "slow difficult task."[3] Even more, we might trick ourselves into thinking we're progressing in our relationship with Christ more than we really are. For we might experience a feeling of closeness with God—a certain joy or delight when pondering his goodness—without taking any steps to put those insights into practice in a way that helps us imitate Christ more.

Taking time out of your day for this kind of prayer—fifteen to twenty to thirty minutes each day—can transform your life. As you fill your mind with Christ's life and prayerfully ponder small ways to live more like him each day, you'll find yourself, with the help of God's grace, slowly being changed, making gradual progress in becoming more like him. You will begin to live more interiorly, more in tune with Christ's Spirit dwelling within you, and more aware of his promptings—and thus more likely to respond to those divine nudges. In this way, Jesus changes us from within so that over time we can say with St. Paul, "It is no longer I who live, but Christ who lives in me" (Gal 2:20).

Do it for your family and friends. Do it for the people you serve. Do it for your own soul. Most of all, do it out of love for the God who so loves you.

---

[3] St. Francis de Sales, *Introduction to the Devout Life*, trans. John K. Ryan (New York: Image, 1989), 89.

I Don't Have Time

One of the biggest excuses people give for not praying each day is the problem of time: "I don't have time. I'm too busy right now." But we always make time for the things we think are important. No one, for example, has died of hunger because they were too busy to take time to eat. No one has ever died of asphyxiation because they were too busy to breathe. Pope Francis said disciples must take in the "deep breath of prayer." Just as we need to breathe in oxygen to live physically, so we need the deep breath of prayer in order to live spiritually.

We all have time. The important question is, what are we doing with it? We make time for the things that we value most. If we value God and our relationship with him, then we will commit some of our time to him each day in prayer. Perhaps we just need to put first things first and ensure that we make prayer a top priority in our day.

Here's an analogy that can help us along these lines. Did you know that if you took three quarters of a cup of beans and three quarters of a cup of rice, you could fit them both in just one cup? Yes, it can be done. But only if you put the beans in first. If you do that, many of the individual grains of rice can fall between the cracks of the beans and take up less space in the one cup. Similarly, if we make our time for prayer a priority, putting it first each day, we'll find that the truly essential things we need to do will somehow still get done. We just have to put God first. "Seek first his kingdom and his righteousness, and all these things shall be yours as well" (Mt 6:33).

Sometimes, however, "I don't have time" is just an excuse. We say we are too busy, but in reality we simply don't want to commit to prayer. We find it too hard, too boring, or too much work. Indeed, meditation demands a lot from us. It's a lot easier to respond to email than it is to sit in the chapel and pray. It's a lot easier to play with our phones, type on our computers, or watch a show than it is to quietly sit with the Bible and meditate on a scene from the Gospels. It's sometimes even easier to pray the Rosary or set prayers from the Liturgy of the Hours than it is to rest in Christ's presence and contemplate his life. While these beautiful prayers and devotions also help deepen one's spiritual life, we want to make sure they don't replace the commitment to daily meditation. Otherwise, we'll easily come up with a hundred excuses for why we need to cut corners on meditative prayer to perform other "urgent" tasks. This, however, is not the heart of a disciple. A true disciple will make his daily encounter with God in meditation a priority, no matter what the cost.

Faithfulness vs. "Good Prayer"

I've heard some people talk about moments when they think their prayer life is going well: "Prayer was really good today." "I had a great time in the chapel." "I got a lot out of my prayer time this morning." "I love doing *lectio divina*." Indeed, there are times when God blesses us with a feeling of his closeness in prayer. We are more aware of his presence, we sense his love, or we get some new insight on a problem we're facing. We should thank the Lord for those moments. But there are also many times when prayer seems dry, when we don't feel God's closeness. Prayer is a drudgery. It's painfully boring. We can't wait for it to be over. We'd rather be doing anything else than sitting quietly with God in prayer. In those moments, when prayer is most challenging, will you still show up?

Far more important than our perceptions about the quality of our prayer is our faithfulness to it each day. Are we consistent with prayer? Are we faithful to Jesus, giving him this time for prayer each day? Even when we don't want to go? Even when we don't think we're getting a lot out of it? God often withdraws the *feelings* of his closeness to test our hearts, to draw out our deepest desires that are for him and not just for the blessings he gives us. He wants to see if we will be faithful even when we don't feel we're getting a lot out of our prayer time.

Real love is not about feelings. And it's not about what we get out of the other person. It's about a commitment to the one we love. I see this in my relationship with my irresistibly cute one-year-old daughter. When she sees me come home from work, she smiles, laughs, and says, "Dada, Dada" as she waddles to the front door to hug me. In those moments, I feel so close to my daughter. As she falls into my arms, I squeeze her tight, kiss her on the cheek, and say, "I love you!"

But when she's sick and wakes up several times in the middle of the night, I don't have those same warm, fuzzy feelings for her. Sadly, there are many other emotions at work at 2:30 in the morning. "I just want a few hours of rest! Why won't you sleep through the night?" But my wife and I still need to love her, serve her, and attend to her—even though we don't get a lot out of it. Imagine if we each said, "Well, there's not much in it for me when she's crying like this—I don't get a lot out of these middle-of-the-night episodes. I don't get good feelings taking care of her at 3:00 a.m., so she's on her own tonight." That's not love. Real love is about *faithfulness*. And the same is true in our relationship with God. True disciples are faithful to God in prayer always, not just when they feel like it or when they think they get

> In those moments, when prayer is most challenging, will you still show up?

a lot out of it. It's about fidelity to Jesus, making time for him each day in prayer and trusting that there's meaning and purpose to our prayer—and that God is still doing good work in our souls, even if we don't feel it.

Reflection Questions

- This chapter addressed the importance of daily meditation. What do you find most challenging or intimidating about that? If Jesus were sitting in the room with you right now, how do you think he'd respond to your concerns about committing to this kind of daily prayer? What would he say to you?

- What is your biggest struggle in praying every day? What's the difference between feeling good about our prayer time and faithfulness to daily prayer? Which is more important?

Conclusion

When pilgrims come to Rome, they cannot help but think of St. Peter. Literally thousands of images related to the Apostle decorate the many churches, museums, buildings, and bridges there. An array of Petrine symbols—keys, fishing boats, fishing nets, a burly bearded man, an upside-down cross—saturate the city. Scenes from his life can be found in paintings, mosaics, and marble statues and etched into walls, ceilings, floors, and windows: Peter on the boat with his brother Andrew. Peter leaving his nets to follow Jesus. Peter walking on the water. Peter getting the keys of the kingdom. Peter witnessing the transfiguration. Peter swimming out into the Sea of Galilee to meet the risen Jesus. Peter preaching at Pentecost. The life of Peter is celebrated throughout the Eternal City because he was the principal leader of the Church in Rome, and this is where the climax of his mission took place: the heroic witness of his martyrdom when he was crucified upside down in Nero's circus.

Peter's life, however, wasn't always worthy of such celebration. There were times he doubted (see Lk 5:1–11), moments he couldn't accept something Jesus said (see

Mt 16:21–23), and times when he completely missed the point of Christ's teachings (see Mt 18:21–22). Then, of course, there were the three times he outright denied Jesus, saying, "I do not know the man."

Indeed, when Jesus first calls him, Peter is far from being the rock he needs to be for the Church. But the son of a carpenter takes the rough material that is Simon the Fisherman, invites him to be a disciple, and begins sculpting him into the foundation for the Church that the gates of Hell can never prevail against (see Mt 16:18). This molding doesn't happen in an instant. And, as we saw in the Introduction, it still isn't complete even when Jesus appears to him after the Resurrection.

But something profound does happen in Peter's post-Easter encounter with Jesus along the Sea of Galilee. This is a key turning point in his life, a defining moment in his ongoing conversion. In this scene, Peter emerges as a changed man. He no longer exhibits the overconfidence and rashness of his youth. His tragic betrayals on Holy Thursday night have left him humbled. So when Jesus asks him, "Do you love me?"—meaning, "Do you love me with *agape* love? Do you love me totally, unconditionally?"—Peter can hardly say yes. Not after what he just did. In this humble moment, Peter comes to realize, at the very core of his being, that he can only offer poor, human, *philia* love. He knows quite acutely that he is incapable of imitating his Master's total, self-giving *agape* love modeled on the Cross.

This fundamental realization of his poverty softens Peter's heart and makes him more malleable in the hands of God. God would send the Spirit into Peter's heart and transform him into the great saint he is known to be today. From this point forward, Peter emerges as a changed man.

In Acts of the Apostles, he's a decisive, confident leader in Jerusalem, but it's a calm confidence rooted now in Christ, not his own ability. After Jesus ascends into Heaven, for example, Peter gathers the other Apostles to choose someone to take Judas's place among the Twelve (see Acts 1:15–26). He then preaches at Pentecost, calling 3,000 people to repentance and Baptism (see Acts 2:1–41). He cures the lame man at the Temple gate (see Acts 3:1–10). And when arrested and interrogated by Caiaphas and the rulers of Jerusalem like Jesus was, Peter does not back down. He does not deny Christ this time. Instead, he courageously proclaims the Gospel to them, even though it brings persecution. This is not the same Peter from the Gospels.

This is a man who has been fundamentally changed. Peter the Disciple is becoming ever more like his Master, Jesus Christ. He is leading like Christ, serving like Christ, preaching like Christ and even suffering like Christ. And the work of the Spirit in Peter's heart will even lead him to share in Christ's sufferings on the Cross when he is crucified like his master at the hands of the Romans. Indeed, the blood of his martyrdom is celebrated as the seed of the Church in Rome.

Not all saints, however, are honored like Peter is. Nor do they need to be. There are many holy men and women of God who never become recognized as canonized saints, yet they have been transformed by Christ just as much as Peter has. So the lesson we all can take away from Peter is about the process of discipleship. What Jesus did in Peter the Fisherman he wants to accomplish in all of us ordinary Christians. He wants to take the raw material of our mundane, imperfect lives and transform us into saints. And that should be very encouraging to us. We want to follow our Lord more closely, but we struggle. We're proud. We're afraid. We're weak. We easily fall back into our old patterns of living. The story of Peter's discipleship, like the story of all the saints, can encourage us: if God can transform Peter, the rough, impulsive fisherman of Galilee, he can transform us as well. Peter's transformation as a disciple reminds us of the hope summed up in the saying "Every saint has a past, and every sinner has a future." May you now shape your future by allowing God to transform you into his likeness as a disciple.

Acknowledgments

I am grateful to the many people in FOCUS (Fellowship of Catholic University Students) with whom I have been blessed to work for the past twenty years not just on the topic of discipleship in theory, but also in practice, on the front lines of evangelization, as the organization forms thousands of people each year to lead others to follow Christ as disciples. Especially during my sabbatical in 2017, several meetings and conversations with FOCUS missionaries provided me with the opportunity to take a closer look at what it means to be a disciple and inspired me to delve deeper into the Scriptures and ponder connections with the saints, the Catholic Tradition, and recent ecclesial teaching on this theme. Special thanks for conversations on this topic go to the following: Curtis Martin, Craig Miller, John Zimmer, Brian McAdam, Kevin Cotter, Daniel Paris, Mark Bartek, Sam Mazzarelli, Nathan Stanley, Jared Smyth, Andy Day, Hilary Draftz, Shannon Zurcher, John Merkle, Marcus Schoch, Carrie Wagner, Brock Martin, John Bishop, Kelsey Bob, and Jeremy Cassidy.

I am also grateful to the Augustine Institute for granting me the sabbatical that afforded me the opportunity for further research on discipleship and for deeper immersion in the FOCUS apostolate this past year. Insights from conversations with my colleagues at the Institute, particularly Christopher Blum, Ben Akers, Douglas Bushman, and Lucas Pollice, also have found their way into the pages of this book. And I'm thankful for our students who participated in the mini-classes on discipleship we did as I was working out the core chapters of the book.

Thanks also go to the pastoral leaders and catechetical experts who have given me valuable feedback as I was working on different parts of the book. Among these are Carole Browne; Anne Langford; Fr. Sean Kilcawley; Fr. Paul Murray, OP; Fr. Frank Donio, SAC; Sr. Marie Kolbe Zamora, FSCC; and Dr. Petroc Willey. I also thank Kyrstyn Bishop for her reviewing the early drafts of the manuscript and her many helpful suggestions. And I'm grateful for Jeff Cole and Grace Hagan for their editorial suggestions that have helped make this a better book.

Most of all, I thank my wife Elizabeth for her support and prayers for this project amid the raising of our children, which, one might argue, is the most basic yet most profound kind of discipleship we lay people can offer.

About the Author

Dr. Edward Sri is a theologian, author, and well-known Catholic speaker who appears regularly on EWTN. Each year he speaks to clergy, parish leaders, catechists, and laity from around the world.

He has written several Catholic best-selling books, including *Men, Women and the Mystery of Love* (Servant); *A Biblical Walk through the Mass* (Ascension); *Walking with Mary* (Image); and *Who Am I to Judge?: Responding to Relativism with Logic and Love* (Augustine Institute–Ignatius Press).

Edward Sri is also the host of the acclaimed film series *Symbolon: The Catholic Faith Explained* (Augustine Institute) and the presenter of several popular faith formation programs, including *A Biblical Walk through the Mass* (Ascension Press); *Mary: A Biblical Walk with the Blessed Mother* (Ascension Press); and *Follow Me: Meeting Jesus in the Gospel of John* (Ascension Press). He also served as the content director for several Augustine Institute sacramental preparation programs, including *Beloved: Finding Happiness in Marriage*; *Forgiven: The Transforming Power of Confession*; and *Reborn: You, Your Child, and the Sacrament of Baptism*.

He is a founding leader with Curtis Martin of FOCUS (Fellowship of Catholic University Students) and currently serves as FOCUS vice president of formation.

Dr. Sri is also the host of the podcast *All Things Catholic* and leads pilgrimages to Rome and the Holy Land each year. He holds a doctorate from the Pontifical University of St. Thomas Aquinas in Rome and is an adjunct professor at the Augustine Institute. He resides with his wife Elizabeth and their eight children in Littleton, Colorado.

You can connect with Edward Sri through his website www.edwardsri.com or follow him on Facebook, Twitter, and Instagram.